WHAT TO-DO
WITH MONEY™

ROBERT MUKES
MINISTRIES

Dedication

This book is dedicated to those who are
willing to learn how to walk in complete victory
in managing money.

A PRACTICAL SPIRITUAL GUIDE FOR MANAGING MONEY GOD'S WAY

WHAT TO-DO WITH MONEY™

By

ROBERT MUKES

CONTENTS

STEWARDSHIP THOUGHTS

The Holy Bible - the Word of God - teaches that all things belong to God, even the silver and gold (Haggai 2:8; Leviticus 27:30; Joshua 6:19; Joel 3:5).

"Behold, the heaven and the heaven of heavens is the Lord's thy God, the earth also, with all that therein is." *(Deuteronomy 10:14)*

This being the case, you have been placed in a position of stewardship (Luke 19:13).

"And God blessed them, and God said unto them, Be fruitful, and multiply, and replenish the earth, and subdue it: and have dominion over the fish of the sea, and over the fowl of the air, and over every living thing that moveth upon the earth." *(Genesis 1:28)*

"Thou madest him to have dominion over the works of thy hands; thou hast put all things under his feet." *(Psalms 8:6)*

"Who hath prevented me, that I should repay him? whatsoever is under the whole heaven is mine." *(Job 41:11)*

Therefore, you must give proper accounting of all things that God places in your trust (Romans 14:12; 1 Corinthians 4:1-2). Bad stewardship is sin in the eyes of God (Matthew 25:14-30).

STEWARDSHIP THOUGHTS

Right priority

You must first give yourself to God - as did the early New Testament churches.

"And all that believed were together, and had all things common; And sold their possessions and goods, and parted them to all men, as every man had need. And they, continuing daily with one accord in the temple, and breaking bread from house to house, did eat their meat with gladness and singleness of heart, Praising God, and having favour with all the people. And the Lord added to the church daily such as should be saved." *(Acts 2:44-47)*

"And the multitude of them that believed were of one heart and of one soul: neither said any of them that ought of the things which he possessed was his own; but they had all things common." *(Acts 4:32)*

"And this they did, not as we hoped, but first gave their own selves to the Lord, and unto us by the will of God." *(2 Corinthians 8:5)*

Then - submit with a teachable spirit (Prov. 13:18). See (Prov. 1:5,5:23,13:13,20:18,21:16;Job 9:4,36:12).

God's deep desire is for you to be a good and faithful steward. Read the parables on handling money in the book of Matthew - chapters 20 and 25.

Biblical Financial Truths

Truth #1

God gives you power to get wealth (Deuteronomy 8:17-20) that you may establish His covenant (Genesis 12:1-3, 17:1-7; Matthew 28:19-20; Ephesians 4:11-16;1 Timothy 2:4; Acts 3:25; Galatians 3:8,9,13,14,29; 1 Thess. 5:23; 2 Thess. 2:13).

Truth #2

"All scripture is given by inspiration of God, and is profitable for doctrine, for reproof, for correction, for instruction in righteousness: That the man of God may be perfect, thoroughly furnished unto all good works."
(2 Timothy 3:16-17)

Truth #3

"For whatsoever things were written aforetime were written for our learning, that we through patience and comfort of the scriptures might have hope."
(Romans 15:4)

Truth #4

"Trust in the Lord with all thine heart; and lean not unto thine own understanding. In all thy ways acknowledge him, and he shall direct thy paths. Be not wise in thine own eyes: fear the Lord, and depart from evil. It shall

be health to thy navel, and marrow to thy bones."
(Proverbs 3:5-8)

Truth #5

"There is a way which seemeth right unto a man, but the end thereof are the ways of death."
(Proverbs 14:12)

Truth #6

"There is no wisdom nor understanding nor counsel against the Lord." *(Proverbs 21:30)*

Man's ways are meaningless without God.

Truth #7

"The Lord knoweth the thoughts of man, that they are vanity. Blessed is the man whom thou chastenest, O Lord, and teachest him out of thy law; That thou mayest give him rest from the days of adversity, until the pit be digged for the wicked."
(Psalms 94:11-13)

Truth #8

"In the house of the righteous is much treasure: but in the revenues of the wicked is trouble." *(Proverbs 15:6)*

There are two ways of approaching the management of money - *man's way* and *God's way*.

WHAT TO-DO WITH MONEY

Man's way. This way is the wrong way. Man's plan will always lead to failure (Proverbs 1:32,12:15, 14:12,17:16 NIV, 28:9,26;Psalms 108:12 NIV, 127:1; 1 Corinthians 2:5-6, 3:19; Luke 12:16-20,16:15).

"And God saw that the wickedness of man was great in the earth, and that every imagination of the thoughts of his heart was only evil continually." *(Genesis 6:5)*

"And God looked upon the earth, and, behold, it was corrupt; for all flesh had corrupted his way upon the earth." *(Genesis 6:12)*

"And it shall come to pass, when many evils and troubles are befallen them, that this song shall testify against them as a witness; for it shall not be forgotten out of the mouths of their seed: for I know their imagination which they go about, even now, before I have brought them into the land which I sware." *(Deuteronomy 31:21)*

"O Lord, I know that the way of man is not in himself: it is not in man that walketh to direct his steps." *(Jeremiah 10:23)*

"Thus saith the Lord; Cursed be the man that trusteth in man, and maketh flesh his arm, and whose heart departeth from the Lord. For he shall be like the heath in the desert, and shall not see when good cometh; but shall inhabit the parched places in the wilderness, in a salt land and not inhabited. The heart is deceitful above all things, and desperately wicked: who can know it." *(Jeremiah 17:5-6,9)*

"All we like sheep have gone astray; we have turned every one to his own way; and the Lord hath laid on him the iniquity of us all." *(Isaiah 53:6)*

"In those days there was no king in Israel, but every man did that which was right in his own eyes." *(Judges 17:6)*

"The wicked, through the pride of his countenance, will not seek after God: God is not in all his thoughts. His ways are always grievous; thy judgments are far above out of his sight: as for all his enemies, he puffeth at them." *(Psalms 10:4-5)*

"The fool hath said in his heart, There is no God. They are corrupt, they have done abominable works, there is none that doeth good. The Lord looked down from heaven upon the children of men, to see if there were any that did understand, and seek God. They are all gone aside, they are all together become filthy: there is none that doeth good, no, not one." *(Psalms 14:1-3)*

"A fool despiseth his father's instruction: but he that regardeth reproof is prudent." *(Proverbs 15:5)*

"There is a way that seemeth right unto a man, but the end thereof are the ways of death."
(Proverbs 16:25)

"The thoughts of the diligent tend only to plenteousness; but of every one that is hasty only to want."
(Proverbs 21:5)

"Commit thy way unto the Lord; trust also in him; and he shall bring it to pass." *(Psalm 37:5)*

Do not put your confidence in the world's way

"Woe to the rebellious children, saith the Lord, that take counsel, but not of me; and that cover with a covering, but not of my spirit, that they may add sin to sin: That walk to go down into Egypt, and have not asked at my mouth; to strengthen themselves in the strength of Pharaoh, and to trust in the shadow of Egypt! Therefore shall the strength of Pharaoh be your shame, and the trust in the shadow of Egypt your confusion." *(Isaiah 30:1-3)*

INTRODUCTION

"The thoughts of the righteous are right: but the counsels of the wicked are deceit. The wicked are overthrown, and are not: but the house of the righteous shall stand." *(Proverbs 12:5,7)*

"They are all gone out of the way, they are together become unprofitable; there is none that doeth good, no, not one. Their throat is an open sepulchre; with their tongues they have used deceit; the poison of asps is under their lips: Whose mouth is full of cursing and bitterness: Their feet are swift to shed blood: Destruction and misery are in their ways."
(Romans 3:12-16)

You don't have the power to change yourself.

"And God saw that the wickedness of man was great in the earth, and that every imagination of the thoughts of his heart was only evil continually."
(Genesis 6:5)

"Who can say, I have made my heart clean, I am pure from my sin?" *(Proverbs 20:9)*

A blinded heart must be regenerated by the power of the blood to walk faithfully with God in the area of finances. See reference. Ephesians 4:17-24

It takes the blood of Jesus.

"And almost all things are by the law purged with blood; and without shedding of blood is no remission." *(Hebrews 9:22)*

"But if we walk in the light, as he is in the light, we have fellowship one with another, and the blood of Jesus Christ his Son cleanseth us from all sin." *(1 John 1:7)*

God destroys worldly wisdom

"Therefore, behold, I will proceed to do a marvellous work among this people, even a marvellous work and a wonder: for the wisdom of their wise men shall perish, and the understanding of their prudent men shall be hid." *(Isaiah 29:14)*

"For it is written, I will destroy the wisdom of the wise, and will bring to nothing the understanding of the prudent." *(1 Corinthians 1:19)*

"Yea also, when he that is a fool walketh by the way, his wisdom faileth him, and he saith to every one that he is a fool." *(Ecclesiastes 10:3)*

See Psalms 33:10 and Isaiah 19:3.

INTRODUCTION

God's way. This is the right way. God's plan will always lead to success (Job 37:16; Psalms 32:8-10,37:5,23,31,34,147:5 NIV; Proverbs 2:1-21,16:9, 20:24,24:7; Isaiah 48:17; Ephesians 1:11; James 1:5;Isaiah 33:6,55:8-9;Hosea 14:9;Revelation 3:18).

Divine wisdom is God's way. This is the ability to apply what you know & understand (Proverbs 15:2,7).

"Through wisdom is an house builded; and by understanding it is established: And by knowledge shall the chambers be filled with all precious and pleasant riches." *(Proverbs 24:3-4)*

"Blessed is the man that trusteth in the Lord, and whose hope the Lord is. For he shall be as a tree planted by the waters, and that spreadeth out her roots by the river, and shall not see when heat cometh, but her leaf shall be green; and shall not be careful in the year of drought, neither shall cease from yielding fruit." *(Jeremiah 17:7-8)*

"And I will set up shepherds over them which shall feed them: and they shall fear no more, nor be dismayed, neither shall they be lacking, saith the Lord." *(Jeremiah 23:4)* Warning ! Romans 13:1-2

"For I know the thoughts that I think toward you, saith the Lord, thoughts of peace, and not of evil, to give you an expected end." *(Jeremiah 29:11)*

"A wise man will hear, and will increase learning; and a man of understanding shall attain unto wise counsels." *(Proverbs 1:5)*

"The wise in heart will receive commandments: but a prating fool shall fall." *(Proverbs 10:8)*

"The thoughts of the righteous are right: but the counsels of the wicked are deceit." *(Proverbs 12:5)*

"The way of a fool is right in his own eyes: but he that hearkeneth unto counsel is wise."
(Proverbs 12:15)

"A wise man feareth, and departeth from evil: but the fool rageth, and is confident." *(Proverbs 14:16)*

"Hear counsel, and receive instruction, that thou mayest be wise in thy latter end. There are many devices in a man's heart; nevertheless the counsel of the Lord, that shall stand." *(Proverbs 19:20-21)*

The Word of God - your example.

"O how love I thy law! it is my meditation all the day. Thou through thy commandments hast made me wiser than mine enemies: for they are ever with me. I have more understanding than all my teachers: for thy testimonies are my meditation. I understand

more than the ancients, because I keep thy precepts. I have refrained my feet from every evil way,
that I might keep thy word. I have not departed from
thy judgments: for thou hast taught me. How sweet
are thy words unto my taste! yea, sweeter than
honey to my mouth! Through thy precepts I get
<u>understanding</u>: therefore I hate every false way."
(Psalms 119:97-104)   See also. Psalms 119:30

Always follow God's plan

Let the one who created you - God - prepare His
plans in your heart by making Him your senior partner.

"The preparations of the heart in man, and the
answer of the tongue, is from the Lord."
(Proverbs 16:1)   To do God's will. Ephesians 6:6

See additional references. Psalms 33:11; Proverbs
3:5-6,19:21; Isaiah 48:17; Matthew 11:29

"Thou shalt guide me with thy counsel, and afterward receive me to glory." *(Psalms 73:24)*

"Except the Lord build the house, they labour in vain
that build it: except the Lord keep the city, the watch-
man waketh but in vain." *(Psalms 127:1)*

In the home. *Men* (Genesis 3:16,18:19; Psalms 37:23-24; Romans 13:1-2; 1 Corinthians 11:3; Ephesians 5:21-25; Colossians 3:19; 1 Peter 3:7-12; 1 Timothy 5:8; Titus 2:2). *Women* (1 Samuel 15:23; Romans 13:1-2; 1 Corinthians 11:3; Ephesians 5:21-24; Titus 2:3-5; Proverbs 9:1, 14:1, 31:10-31; Colossians 3:18; 1 Timothy 5:8; Isaiah 3:12; 1 Kings 21:25). *Unity* (Amos 3:3; 1 Peter 5:5; 1 Peter 2:13-15,3:5-7; Exodus 22:28; Acts 23:4-5).

The assurance of God's Word.

God can't lie

"God is not a man, that he should lie; neither the son of man, that he should repent: hath he said, and shall he not do it? or hath he spoken, and shall he not make it good." *(Numbers 23:19)*

"So shall my word be that goeth forth out of my mouth: it shall not return unto me void, but it shall accomplish that which I please, and it shall prosper in the thing whereto I sent it." *(Isaiah 55:11)*

God is faithful

"Know therefore that the Lord thy God, he is God, the faithful God, which keepeth covenant and mercy with them that love him and keep his command-ments to a thousand generations."
(Deuteronomy 7:9)

INTRODUCTION

God expects you to be faithful.

"Moreover it is required in stewards, that a man be found faithful." *(1 Corinthians 4:2)*

See other references on being a good steward. Romans 14:12; 1 Corinthians 4:2,7:30,11:31-32; Hebrews 4:12; 1 John 2:17

You must walk in the assurance of God's Word, like Paul did.

"For the which cause I also suffer these things: nevertheless I am not ashamed: for I know whom I have believed, and am persuaded that he is able to keep that which I have committed unto him against that day." *(2 Timothy 1:12)*

By the way, God doesn't need any money.

"The silver is mine, and the gold is mine, saith the Lord of hosts." *(Haggai 2:8)*   See also. Job 41:11

"For every beast of the forest is mine, and the cattle upon a thousand hills. I know all the fowls of the mountains: and the wild beasts of the field are mine. If I were hungry, I would not tell thee: for the world is mine, and the fulness thereof." *(Psalms 50:10-12)*

"God that made the world and all things therein, seeing that he is Lord of heaven and earth, dwelleth not in temples made with hands; Neither is worshipped with men's hands, as though he needed any thing, seeing he giveth to all life, and breath, and all things." *(Acts 17:24-25)*

"John answered and said, A man can receive nothing, except it be given him from heaven." *(John 3:27)*

God seeks your salvation not your things

Paul's 2nd letter to the Church @ Corinth

"Behold, the third time I am ready to come to you; and I will not be burdensome to you: for I seek not yours, but you: for the children ought not to lay up for the parents, but the parents for the children. And I will very gladly spend and be spent for you; though the more abundantly I love you, the less I be loved. But be it so, I did not burden you: nevertheless, being crafty, I caught you with guile. Did I make a gain of you by any of them whom I sent unto you? I desired Titus, and with him I sent a brother. Did Titus make a gain of you? walked we not in the same spirit? walked we not in the same steps?" *(2 Corinthians 12:14-18)*

Don't forget God's warning.

"When thou hast eaten and art full, then thou shalt bless the Lord thy God for the good land which he hath given thee. Beware that thou forget not the Lord thy God, in not keeping his commandments,

INTRODUCTION

and his judgments, and his statutes, which I command thee this day: Lest when thou hast eaten and art full, and hast built goodly houses, and dwelt therein; And when thy herds and thy flocks multiply, and thy silver and thy gold is multiplied, and all that thou hast is multiplied; Then thine heart be lifted up, and thou forget the Lord thy God, which brought thee forth out of the land of Egypt, from the house of bondage; Who led thee through that great and terrible wilderness, wherein were fiery serpents, and scorpions, and drought, where there was no water; who brought thee forth water out of the rock of flint; Who fed thee in the wilderness with manna, which thy fathers knew not, that he might humble thee, and that he might prove thee, to do thee good at thy latter end; And thou say in thine heart, My power and the might of mine hand hath gotten me this wealth. But thou shalt remember the Lord thy God: for it is he that giveth thee power to get wealth, that he may establish his covenant which he sware unto thy fathers, as it is this day. And it shall be, if thou do at all forget the Lord thy God, and walk after other gods, and serve them, and worship them, I testify against you this day that ye shall surely perish. As the nations which the Lord destroyeth before your face, so shall ye perish; because ye would not be obedient unto the voice of the Lord your God." *(Deuteronomy 8:10-20)*

"Woe to the rebellious children, saith the Lord, that take counsel, but not of me; and that cover with a covering, but not of my spirit, that they may add sin to sin: That walk to go down into Egypt, and have not asked at my mouth; to strengthen themselves in the strength of Pharaoh, and to trust in the shadow of Egypt! Therefore shall the strength of Pharaoh be your shame, and the trust in the shadow of Egypt your confusion." *(Isaiah 30:1-3)*

God's way is with a teachable spirit
This is the key to God's blessings

"Poverty and shame shall be to him that refuseth instruction: but he that regardeth reproof shall be honoured." *(Proverbs 13:18)*

"Teach me thy way, O Lord; I will walk in thy truth: unite my heart to fear thy name." *(Psalms 86:11)*

"Commit thy works unto the Lord, and thy thoughts shall be established." *(Proverbs 16:3)*

"I can do all things through Christ which strength-eneth me." *(Philippians 4:13)*

See additional references. Proverbs 15:33,22:4, 29:23; Daniel 4:37; Matthew 5:3; 1 Peter 5:5

INTRODUCTION

Which way will you follow ?

"Blessed is the man who does not walk in the counsel of the wicked or stand in the way of sinners or sit in the seat of mockers. But his delight is in the law of the LORD, and on his law he meditates day and night. For the LORD watches over the way of the righteous, but the way of the wicked will perish." *(Psalms 1:1,2,6 NIV)*

See also. Proverbs 4:18-19,12:5,15:9,22

This revelation will not profit you - if you do not mix it with faith

"For unto us was the gospel preached, as well as unto them: but the word preached did not profit them, not being mixed with faith in them that heard it." *(Hebrews 4:2)*

"But be ye doers of the word, and not hearers only, deceiving your own selves." *(James 1:22)*

Remember

"The steps of a good man are ordered by the Lord: and he delighteth in his way." *(Psalms 37:23)*

The counsel of God shall stand (Isaiah 46:10). He will guide you in the right way (Psalms 18:30,32) - continually (Isaiah 58:11) by His Spirit (John 16:13). God's way is perfect - He is the one to make your way perfect (2 Samuel 22:31,33).

CHAPTER 1

Principle #1

ACQUIRE IT HONESTLY

God's principles of honesty must be followed when acquiring money. You must learn to pass God's test of honesty.

Words of Jeremiah on getting riches

"As the partridge sitteth on eggs, and hatcheth them not; so he that getteth riches, and not by right, shall leave them in the midst of his days, and at his end shall be a fool." *(Jeremiah 17:11)*

Words of Job on getting riches

"This is the portion of a wicked man with God, and the heritage of oppressors, which they shall receive of the Almighty. Though he heap up silver as the dust, and prepare raiment as the clay; He may prepare it, but the just shall put it on, and the innocent shall divide the silver." *(Job 27:13,16,17)*

ACQUIRE IT HONESTLY

"Ye shall not steal, neither deal falsely, neither lie one to another. And ye shall not swear by my name falsely, neither shalt thou profane the name of thy God: I am the Lord. Thou shalt not defraud thy neighbour, neither rob him: the wages of him that is hired shall not abide with thee all night until the morning." *(Leviticus 19:11-13)*

"In those days there was no king in Israel, but every man did that which was right in his own eyes." *(Judges 17:6)*

Words of Solomon on getting riches

"Wealth gotten by vanity shall be diminished: but he that gathereth by labour shall increase." *(Proverbs 13:11)*

Vanity (Unrighteous labor, not earned, meaning- less, unsatisfactory).

"The getting of treasures by a lying tongue is a van- ity tossed to and fro of them that seek death." *(Proverbs 21:6)* See also. Proverbs 15:6

One of the reasons why Satan fell is because of dishonest gain (Ezekiel 28:12-18).

Example of dishonest gain. Lying - 2 Kings 5:20-27. Example of honest gain. Sowing - Genesis 26:12.

"Lying lips are abomination to the Lord: but they that deal truly are his delight." *(Proverbs 12:22)*

"Divers weights are an abomination unto the Lord; and a false balance is not good." *(Proverbs 20:23)*

"He that by usury and unjust gain increaseth his substance, he shall gather it for him that will pity the poor." *(Proverbs 28:8)*

Words of Apostle Paul

"Recompense to no man evil for evil. Provide things honest in the sight of all men." *(Romans 12:17)*

"Let him that stole steal no more: but rather let him labour, working with his hands the thing which is good, that he may have to give to him that needeth." *(Ephesians 4:28)*

Additional references on acquiring money honestly. Genesis 2:15,3:19;26:12;Exodus 20:9;Psalms 10:3; Deuteronomy 25:15; 2 Thessalonians 3:10,11; Proverbs 6:6,10:2-3,11:1,12:11,16:8,20:4,22:16,29, 28:19; Jeremiah 22:13; Mark 10:17-27; Luke 16:10; Acts 24:16; 1 Thessalonians 4:11-12; Romans 12:9-21; 2 Thessalonians 3:7-9; 1 Timothy 2:2; Proverbs 3:9 AMP - Capital by righteous labor

God will remember how you obtained your money (Amos 8:5-7).

ACQUIRE IT HONESTLY

You don't have to do anything sinful for God to meet your needs. He has already made provisions to meet your every need (**Matthew 6:26**; **2 Corinthians 9:8**). You don't have to sale drugs (Matt. 27:6), sale your body (Deut. 23:18), gamble, lie, steal, kill, make merchandise of people or serve the devil in any way to walk in the promises of God (Jer. 25:6-7; 2 Peter 2:3; Psalms 23:1,33:18-21,37:5,7,40:1,121:1-2).

The Word of God teaches you God's provisions for meeting your needs and even giving you the desires of your heart, once you learn how to delight yourself in Him (Psalms 34:9-10,37:3,4,19,55:22,84:11,89:33;Job 36:11;Prov. 10:3, 28:20).

God's ways of meeting your needs (Heb. 10:35-36)
If you meet His covenant conditions (*Be in His family*)
(Gen. 17:1-7; Matt. 6:31-33; Gal. 3:13-14,29)
(*Serve Him* - Matthew 6:24; *Seek Him first* - Matthew 6:33, Prov. 3:5-6, Isaiah 48:17; *Faithful Steward* - Luke 16:10-12; *Support God's work* - Malachi 3:10-11, Luke 6:38, 2 Cor. 8:7, 9:6-8,Philippians 4:14-19;*Right Motives* - James 4:3; *Fear God* - Psalms 34:9; *Patience* - Romans 4:21,5:3-5)
- **Your Job** (talents/natural gifts) Deut. 30:8-10; Prov. 10:4, 12:11,14, 13:11, 28:19; Eccl. 9:10; Ex. 36:1-4; 2 Pet. 1:10; Jer. 25:6-7; Col. 3:23-24; 2 Chr. 15:7; 1 Thess. 4:11-12.
- **Own Business** Luke 14:28;Prov. 15:22;Isaiah 48:17,58:11.
- **Ministry Office** Eph. 4:11,12; 1 Cor. 9:7-14; Gal. 6:6.
- **Your Natural Family** 1 Timothy 5:8; Proverbs 13:22; 1 Timothy 5:4; 2 Corinthians 12:14.
- **Your Spiritual Family** Acts 2:41-45, Acts 4:31-35; Acts 11:29; Galatians 6:10;1 John 3:17; Romans 15:25-26.
- **Uncommon Blessings** James 1:17; Exodus 11:2-3; Job 42:10-15; Matthew 14:18-21,17:27; 1 Kings 17:9-16; Psalms 78:23-25; Prov. 8:12; Eccl. 11:5; Ephesians 3:20.
- **Inheritance of the Heathen** Psalms 2:8; Eccl. 2:26.
- **Investment Income** Eccl. 11:2; Matt. 25:27; Luke 19:11-26.

CHAPTER 2

Principle #2

HONOR GOD

This is to glorify God (even in giving - 1 Peter 4:11; 1 Corinthians 10:31).

To remember God's goodness with your giving

Words of David

"Wherefore David blessed the Lord before all the congregation: and David said, Blessed be thou, Lord God of Israel our father, for ever and ever. Thine, O Lord, is the greatness, and the power, and the glory, and the victory, and the majesty: for all that is in the heaven and in the earth is thine; thine is the kingdom, O Lord, and thou art exalted as head above all. Both riches and honour come of thee, and thou reignest over all; and in thine hand is power and might; and in thine hand it is to make great, and to give strength unto all. Now therefore, our God, we thank thee, and praise thy glorious name. But who am I, and what is my people, that we should be able to offer so willingly after this sort? for all things come of thee, and of thine own have we given thee."
(1 Chronicles 29:10-14)

HONOR GOD

"And all the tithe of the land, whether of the seed of the land, or of the fruit of the tree, is the Lord's: it is holy unto the Lord." *(Leviticus 27:30)*

"And thou shalt speak and say before the Lord thy God, A Syrian ready to perish was my father, and he went down into Egypt, and sojourned there with a few, and became there a nation, great, mighty, and populous: And the Egyptians evil entreated us, and afflicted us, and laid upon us hard bondage: And when we cried unto the Lord God of our fathers, the Lord heard our voice, and looked on our affliction, and our labour, and our oppression: And the Lord brought us forth out of Egypt with a mighty hand, and with an outstretched arm, and with great terribleness, and with signs, and with wonders: And he hath brought us into this place, and hath given us this land, even a land that floweth with milk and honey. And now, behold, I have brought the firstfruits of the land, which thou, O Lord, hast given me. And thou shalt set it before the Lord thy God, and worship before the Lord thy God."
(Deuteronomy 26:5-10)

You honor (glorify) God, when you do what He tells you to do (John 17:4). If you disobey, you are taking away His glory (Isaiah 43:7; Romans 3:23).

"Honour the Lord with thy substance, and with the firstfruits of all thine increase: So shall thy barns be filled with plenty, and thy presses shall burst out with new wine." *(Proverbs 3:9-10)*

"Bring ye all the tithes into the storehouse, that there may be meat in mine house, and prove me now herewith, saith the Lord of hosts, if I will not open you the windows of heaven, and pour you out a blessing, that there shall not be room enough to receive it. And I will rebuke the devourer for your sakes, and he shall not destroy the fruits of your ground; neither shall your vine cast her fruit before the time in the field, saith the Lord of hosts."
(Malachi 3:10-11)

Honoring God this way glorifies Him

"For the administration of this service not only sup-plieth the want of the saints, but is abundant also by many thanksgivings unto God; Whiles by the exper-iment of this ministration they glorify God for your professed subjection into the gospel of Christ, and for your liberal distribution unto them, and unto all men." *(2 Corinthians 9:12-13)*

Ascribing glory to God is the key to your spiritual growth (2 Peter 3:18; Luke 16:11).

HONOR GOD

"But whoso hath this world's good, and seeth his brother have need, and shutteth up his bowels of compassion from him, how dwelleth the love of God in him? My little children, let us not love in word, neither in tongue; but in deed and in truth. And hereby we know that we are of the truth, and shall assure our hearts before him." *(1 John 3:17-19)*

This is proof of being a Christian. The money doesn't glorify God. The act of obedience glorifies Him.

Honoring God in supporting the work of the ministry is well pleasing to God.

"Notwithstanding ye have well done, that ye did communicate with my affliction. Now ye Philippians know also, that in the beginning of the gospel, when I departed from Macedonia, no church communicated with me as concerning giving and receiving, but ye only. For even in Thessalonica ye sent once and again unto my necessity. Not because I desire a gift: but I desire fruit that may abound to your account. But I have all, and abound: I am full, having received of Epaphroditus the things which were sent from you, an odour of a sweet smell, a sacrifice acceptable, wellpleasing to God."
(Philippians 4:14-18)

Read Romans 13:7.

CHAPTER 3
Principle #3
BUDGET

Many believe that budgeting limits God's ability to show himself strong in their lives. However, this part of financial stewardship allows you to better manage God's given resources, and it glorifies Him. Remember, if your earthly net worth is greater than your heavenly net worth, your account with God is out of balance and desperately needs reconciling.

Solomon's perspective on budgeting

"A false balance is abomination to the Lord: but a just weight is his delight." *(Proverbs 11:1)*

"Except the Lord build the house, they labour in vain that build it: except the Lord keep the city, the watch-man waketh but in vain." *(Psalms 127:1)*

"Be thou diligent to know the state of thy flocks, and look well to thy herds." *(Proverbs 27:23)*

Paul's perspective on budgeting

"But he that is spiritual judgeth all things, yet he him-self is judged of no man." *(1 Corinthians 2:15)*

BUDGET

A parable of Jesus, of the necessity, of His follow-ers counting up the cost.

"For which of you, intending to build a tower, sitteth not down first, and counteth the cost, whether he have sufficient to finish it? Lest haply, after he hath laid the foundation, and is not able to finish it, all that behold it begin to mock him, Saying, This man began to build, and was not able to finish."
(Luke 14:28-30)

Not counting the cost is rebellion against God.

8 Steps to Biblical Budgeting

1. Pray for wisdom.
2. Determine your monthly income.
3. Pay God tithes (10%) & give an offering.
4. Determine your fixed monthly expenses.
5. Determine your variable monthly expenses.
6. Determine your debts (secured & unsecured).
7. Determine your investments & savings.
8. Reconcile your monthly budget.

See additional references on budgeting. Proverbs 16:11,20:10,23,22:3,24:3-4; Micah 6:11; Matthew 18:23-35,25:14-30; Luke 12:16-21,16:1-8; 1 Corinthians 16:1-2; John 6:12

CHAPTER 4
Principle #4

HELP SUPPORT GOD'S WORK

Help support God's work, through the ministry of giving. Always be mindful - that God is the object of giving. When you support God's Work, you are: (1)Blessing God Himself (Matthew 25:31-46); (2) Helping to save the souls of others (1 Corinthians 10:31,33); (3) Laying up treasures in heaven (Matthew 6:19-21); (4) Obeying God's law (1 Corinthians 9:8). Remember, God will not forget all your support (Psalms 35:27-28; Jer. 17:10; Heb. 6:10).

God's overall plan

To establish His kingdom over all the earth(Psalms 110:1-3)

"But thou shalt remember the Lord thy God: for it is he that giveth thee power to get wealth, that he may establish his covenant which he sware unto thy fathers, as it is this day." *(Deuteronomy 8:18)*

"And he said unto them, Go ye into all the world, and preach the gospel to every creature." *(Mark 16:15)*

"Who will have all men to be saved, and to come unto the knowledge of the truth." *(1 Timothy 2:4)*

"For we are his workmanship, created in Christ Jesus unto good works, which God hath before ordained that we should walk in them."
(Ephesians 2:10)

"But whoso hath this world's good, and seeth his brother have need, and shutteth up his bowels of compassion from him, how dwelleth the love of God in him?   My little children, let us not love in word, neither in tongue; but in deed and in truth."
(1 John 3:17-18)

When you support the work of the ministry, God promises to bless you with natural dividends and spiritual dividends.

Natural dividends (earthly blessings)

"Give, and it shall be given unto you; good measure, pressed down, and shaken together, and running over, shall men give into your bosom. For with the same measure that ye mete withal it shall be measured to you again." *(Luke 6:38)* Matt. 19:29; 2 Cor. 9:7-8

Spiritual dividends (heavenly blessings)

"Not because I desire a gift: but I desire fruit that may abound to your account." *(Philippians 4:17)*   See also. 1 Peter 1:3-4

The fruit added to your heavenly account represents good works and deeds written in the book of remembrance (Malachi 3:16). True wealth is not based upon your natural portfolio - it is based upon your spiritual portfolio (Matthew 6:19-20).

Other references. Psalms 144:3; 1 Peter 4:5; Mark 10:21; 2 Corinthians 9:6; Mark 10:29-30;Galatians 6:7; Malachi 3:10

WHAT TO-DO WITH MONEY

Areas of Support

Restoring the desolate houses of God

"Now when all this was finished, all Israel that were present went out to the cities of Judah, and brake the images in pieces, and cut down the groves, and threw down the high places and the altars out of all Judah and Benjamin, in Ephraim also and Manasseh, until they had utterly destroyed them all. Then all the children of Israel returned, every man to his possession, into their own cities.

And Hezekiah appointed the courses of the priests and the Levites after their courses, every man according to his service, the priests and Levites for burnt offerings and for peace offerings, to minister, and to give thanks, and to praise in the gates of the tents of the Lord. He appointed also the king's portion of his substance for the burnt offerings, to wit, for the morning and evening burnt offerings, and the burnt offerings for the sabbaths, and for the new moons, and for the set feasts, as it is written in the law of the Lord. Moreover he commanded the people that dwelt in Jerusalem to give the portion of the priests and the Levites, that they might be encouraged in the law of the Lord.

And as soon as the commandment came abroad, the children of Israel brought in abundance the firstfruits of corn, wine, and oil, and honey, and of all the increase of the field; and the tithe of all things brought they in abundantly. And concerning the children of Israel and Judah, that dwelt in the cities of Judah, they also brought in the tithe of oxen and sheep, and the tithe of holy things which were consecrated unto the Lord their God, and laid them by heaps. In the third month they began to lay the foundation of the heaps, and finished them in the seventh month. And when Hezekiah and the princes came and saw the heaps, they blessed the Lord, and his people Israel. Then Hezekiah questioned with the priests and the Levites concerning the heaps. And Azariah the chief priest of the house of Zadok answered him, and said, Since the people began to bring the offerings into the house of the Lord, we have had enough to eat, and have left plenty: for the Lord hath blessed his people; and that which is left is this great store.

Then Hezekiah commanded to prepare chambers in the house of the Lord; and they prepared them, And brought in the offerings and the tithes and the dedicated things faithfully: over which Cononiah the Levite was ruler, and Shimei his brother was the next. And Jehiel, and Azaziah, and Nahath, and Asahel, and Jerimoth, and Jozabad, and Eliel, and Ismachiah, and Mahath, and Benaiah, were overseers under the hand of Cononiah and Shimei his brother, at the commandment of Hezekiah the king, and Azariah the ruler of the house of God.   And

WHAT TO-DO WITH MONEY

Kore the son of Imnah the Levite, the porter toward the east, was over the freewill offerings of God, to distribute the oblations of the Lord, and the most holy things. And next him were Eden, and Miniamin, and Jeshua, and Shemaiah, Amariah, and Shecaniah, in the cities of the priests, in their set office, to give to their brethren by courses, as well to the great as to the small: Beside their genealogy of males, from three years old and upward, even unto every one that entereth into the house of the Lord, his daily portion for their service in their charges according to their courses; Both to the genealogy of the priests by the house of their fathers, and the Levites from twenty years old and upward, in their charges by their courses; And to the genealogy of all their little ones, their wives, and their sons, and their daughters, through all the congregation: for in their set office they sanctified themselves in holiness: Also of the sons of Aaron the priests, which were in the fields of the suburbs of their cities, in every several city, the men that were expressed by name, to give portions to all the males among the priests, and to all that were reckoned by genealogies among the Levites.

And thus did Hezekiah throughout all Judah, and wrought that which was good and right and truth before the Lord his God. And in every work that he began in the service of the house of God, and in the

law, and in the commandments, to seek his God, he did it with all his heart, and prospered."
(2 Chronicles 31:1-21) **See. 2 Kings 12:4-15, 22:1-5**

In the building of God's house

"Take ye from among you an offering unto the Lord: whosoever is of a willing heart, let him bring it, an offering of the Lord; gold, and silver, and brass, And blue, and purple, and scarlet, and fine linen, and goats' hair, And rams' skins dyed red, and badgers' skins, and shittim wood, And oil for the light, and spices for anointing oil, and for the sweet incense, And onyx stones, and stones to be set for the ephod, and for the breastplate. And every wise hearted among you shall come, and make all that the Lord hath commanded; And they came, every one whose heart stirred him up, and every one whom his spirit made willing, and they brought the Lord's offering to the work of the tabernacle of the congregation, and for all his service, and for the holy garments. And they came, both men and women, as many as were willing hearted, and brought bracelets, and earrings, and rings, and tablets, all jewels of gold: and every man that offered offered an offering of gold unto the Lord." *(Exodus 35:5-10,21,22)*

In Matthew 10:37, Jesus says He is number one.

WHAT TO-DO WITH MONEY

David put God's house first

"Moreover, because I have set my affection to the house of my God, I have of mine own proper good, of gold and silver, which I have given to the house of my God, over and above all that I have prepared for the holy house." *(1 Chronicles 29:3)*

Why build a building ?
Exodus 25:8-9; Hebrews 10:25

To compel people to come in - that God's house may be full. Not by using worldly means - but simply lifting up the name of Jesus (John 12:32).

"And the lord said unto the servant, Go out into the highways and hedges, and compel them to come in, that my house may be filled." *(Luke 14:23)*

God wants you to support His work with money.

"And they came, both men and women, as many as were willing hearted, and brought bracelets, and earrings, and rings, and tablets, all jewels of gold: and every man that offered offered an offering of gold unto the Lord." *(Exodus 35:22)*

See additional reference. 2 Chronicles 31:11-12

HELP SUPPORT GOD'S WORK

Additional references on supporting God's work with money.

• Tabernacle. Exodus 25:1-2; 36:3
• First Temple. 1 Chronicles 22:14,28:12,19,29:4,7
• Second Temple. Ezra 1:1-4,2:64-68,3:7
• Support from unbelievers. Ex. 11:2-3; Rom. 15:27
• Jesus' ministry. Luke 8:1-3
• Early Church.   Acts 4:32-37; 1 Corinthians 9:7-14

Maintaining the house of God (kingdom of God)
By replenishing God's house

"Bring ye all the tithes into the storehouse, that there may be meat in mine house, and prove me now herewith, saith the Lord of hosts, if I will not open you the windows of heaven, and pour you out a blessing, that there shall not be room enough to receive it." *(Malachi 3:10)*

"And the priest the son of Aaron shall be with the Levites, when the Levites take tithes: and the Levites shall bring up the tithe of the tithes unto the house of our God, to the chambers, into the treasure house. For the children of Israel and the children of Levi shall bring the offering of the corn, of the new wine, and the oil, unto the chambers, where are the vessels of the sanctuary, and the priests that minister, and the porters, and the singers: and we will not forsake the house of our God." *(Nehemiah 10:38-39)*

Additional references. 2 Kings 12:7-9;Numbers <u>7:1-5</u>; Nehemiah 10:32; Leviticus <u>24:1-2</u>; Ezekiel <u>44:30</u>; 1 Chronicles 26:27

Building up the local church by supporting pastors and the five-fold ministry

Pastors: Feeding and shepherding the sheep

"And I will give you pastors according to mine heart, which shall feed you with knowledge and under-standing." *(Jeremiah 3:15)*

Additional references. Jeremiah 23:4; John 10:7-16

"Who goeth a warfare any time at his own charges? who planteth a vineyard, and eateth not of the fruit thereof? or who feedeth a flock, and eateth not of the milk of the flock? Say I these things as a man? or saith not the law the same also? For it is written in the law of Moses, Thou shalt not muzzle the mouth of the ox that treadeth out the corn. Doth God take care for oxen? Or saith he it altogether for our sakes? For our sakes, no doubt, this is written: that he that ploweth should plow in hope; and that he that thresheth in hope should be partaker of his hope." *(1 Corinthians 9:7-10)*

"Let him that is taught in the word communicate unto him that teacheth in all good things." *(Galatians 6:6)*

Five-fold ministry: Ephesians 4:11-14

HELP SUPPORT GOD'S WORK

See other references for support of ministry workers. Deuteronomy 25:4; 1 Timothy 5:17-19; 2 Timothy 2:6; Matthew 10:9-11; Luke 10:7; Hebrews 7:1-10, 13:7,10,17; 1 Cor. 9:7-14; 2 Cor. 11:7-9; Romans 15:27. To keep people from ending up in hell (Rev. 21:7-8).

Building up the body of Christ
By supporting evangelistic/missionary ministries

Send forth the laborers (Luke 10:2)

"And this gospel of the kingdom shall be preached in all the world for a witness unto all nations; and then shall the end come." *(Matthew 24:14)*

"Moreover, brethren, we do you to wit of the grace of God bestowed on the churches of Macedonia; How that in a great trial of affliction the abundance of their joy and their deep poverty abounded unto the riches of their liberality. For to their power, I bear record, yea, and beyond their power they were willing of themselves; Praying us with much intreaty that we would receive the gift, and take upon us the fellowship of the ministering to the saints."
(2 Corinthians 8:1-4)

"For we stretch not ourselves beyond our measure, as though we reached not unto you: for we are come as far as to you also in preaching the gospel of Christ: To preach the gospel in the regions beyond you, and not to boast in another man's line of things made ready to our hand." *(2 Corinthians 10:14,16)*

See the following additional references for support of evangelistic work in the kingdom of God through the substance of the saints. Mark 16:15; Luke 8:1-3; Acts 4:32,34-37; 1 Corinthians 16:2; Romans 12:13,15:27; 2 Corinthians 8:4; Ephesians 4:11-15; Philippians 4:15-18; 2 Thessalonians 3:7-9; Galatians 6:10; Acts 11:29; 2 Kings 4:8; 3 John 5-8. Why support God's work ? Romans 10:17,1:16

God promises mercy for those who show mercy toward others (Psalms 37:21, 112:9; Matthew 5:7; 2 Corinthians 9:9; Psalms 41:1-3).

God's promise to those who put His house first

In the following words of God, He challenges you to prove (test - examine - try) Him.

"Bring ye all the tithes into the storehouse, that there may be meat in mine house, and prove me now herewith, saith the Lord of hosts, if I will not open you the windows of heaven, and pour you out a blessing, that there shall not be room enough to receive it. And I will rebuke the devourer for your sakes, and he shall not destroy the fruits of your ground; neither shall your vine cast her fruit before the time in the field, saith the Lord of hosts. And all nations shall call you blessed: for ye shall be a delightsome land, saith the Lord of hosts."
(Malachi 3:10-12)

HELP SUPPORT GOD'S WORK

Blessing reminder !

God's promise to those who do not put His house first

"Then came the word of the Lord by Haggai the prophet, saying, Is it time for you, O ye, to dwell in your cieled houses, and this house lie waste? Now therefore thus saith the Lord of hosts; Consider your ways. Ye have sown much, and bring in little; ye eat, but ye have not enough; ye drink, but ye are not filled with drink; ye clothe you, but there is none warm; and he that earneth wages earneth wages to put it into a bag with holes.

Thus saith the Lord of hosts; Consider your ways. Go up to the mountain, and bring wood, and build the house; and I will take pleasure in it, and I will be glorified, saith the Lord. Ye looked for much, and, lo, it came to little; and when ye brought it home, I did blow upon it. Why? saith the Lord of hosts. Because of mine house that is waste, and ye run every man unto his own house. Therefore the heaven over you is stayed from dew, and the earth is stayed from her fruit. And I called for a drought upon the land, and upon the mountains, and upon the corn, and upon the new wine, and upon the oil, and upon that which the ground bringeth forth, and upon men, and upon cattle, and upon all the labour of the hands."
(Haggai 1:3-11)   See. Haggai 1:12,14, 2:5-9,18,19

WHAT TO-DO WITH MONEY

God's primary ways of support

Offering. This word comes from the Hebrew words Teruwmah or Ter-oo-maw' Strong's 8641 and Ruwm 7311. This is a holy sacrificial gift or present that is *given* to God with a willing heart.

"And Moses spake unto all the congregation of the children of Israel, saying, This is the thing which the Lord commanded, saying, Take ye from among you an offering unto the Lord: whosoever is of a willing heart, let him bring it, an offering of the Lord; gold, and silver, and brass; And they came, every one whose heart stirred him up, and every one whom his spirit made willing, and they brought the Lord's offering to the work of the tabernacle of the congregation, and for all his service, and for the holy garments."
(Exodus 35:4,5,21)

"And thither ye shall bring your burnt offerings, and your sacrifices, and your tithes, and heave offerings of your hand, and your vows, and your freewill offerings, and the firstlings of your herds and of your flocks: Then there shall be a place which the Lord your God shall choose to cause his name to dwell there; thither shall ye bring all that I command you; your burnt offerings, and your sacrifices, your tithes, and the heave offering of your hand, and all your choice vows which ye vow unto the Lord."
(Deuteronomy 12:6,11)

HELP SUPPORT GOD'S WORK

Before the Mosaic law

"And in process of time it came to pass, that Cain brought of the fruit of the ground an offering unto the Lord. And Abel, he also brought of the firstlings of his flock and of the fat thereof. And the Lord had respect unto Abel and to his offering: But unto Cain and to his offering he had not respect. And Cain was very wroth, and his countenance fell."
(Genesis 4:3-5) See also. Hebrews 11:4

During the Mosaic law

Making of the tabernacle

"And the Lord spake unto Moses, saying, Speak unto the children of Israel, that they bring me an offering: of every man that giveth it willingly with his heart ye shall take my offering. And this is the offering which ye shall take of them; gold, and silver, and brass." *(Exodus 25:1-3)* See also. Numbers 7:1-5

"Will a man rob God? Yet ye have robbed me. But ye say, Wherein have we robbed thee? In tithes and offerings." *(Malachi 3:8)*

See additional references. 1 Samuel 2:36; 2 Kings 12:7-9;2 Chronicles 31:11-12 (taken to God's house) Offering of firstfruits. Deuteronomy 26:10

WHAT TO-DO WITH MONEY

Jesus' earthly ministry and after the Mosaic law

"Therefore if thou bring thy gift to the altar, and there rememberest that thy brother hath ought against thee; Leave there thy gift before the altar, and go thy way; first be reconciled to thy brother, and then come and offer thy gift." *(Matthew 5:23-24)*

See additional references.   Matthew 8:1-4; Luke 8:1-3, 6:38; John 13:29; Leviticus 22:21

The early church (Acts 4:31-35, 5:1-11; 1 Corinthians 9:8; 1 Corinthians 16:1-3; 2 Corinthians 9:10-12; Philippians 4:18; Hebrews 13:16). The future eternal temple (Psalms 68:29-32, 72:9-11; Ezekiel 43:7; Zechariah 6:12-13).

Tithe. This word comes from the Hebrew words Ma`aser or Mah-as-ayr', strongs 4643 & `Asar, strongs 6240. A tenth of all increases *paid* to God.

"Notwithstanding no devoted thing, that a man shall devote unto the Lord of all that he hath, both of man and beast, and of the field of his possession, shall be sold or redeemed: every devoted thing is most holy unto the Lord. None devoted, which shall be devoted of men, shall be redeemed; but shall surely be put to death.   And all the tithe of the land, whether of the seed of the land, or of the fruit of the tree, is the Lord's: it is holy unto the Lord.   And if a man will at all redeem ought of his tithes, he shall add thereto the fifth part thereof. And concerning the tithe of the herd, or of the flock, even of whatsoever passeth under the rod, the <u>tenth</u> shall be holy unto the Lord. He shall not search whether it be good or bad, <u>neither shall he change it</u>: and if he change it at all, then both it and the change thereof shall be holy; it shall not be redeemed. These are the commandments, which the Lord commanded Moses for the children of Israel in mount Sinai." *(Leviticus 27:28-34)*   See also. 1 Samuel 8:15,17

See additional reference. Deuteronomy 14:22-26; Malachi 3:8

Every Christian doctrine must be proved by two or more biblical references to be binding.

"This is the third time I am coming to you. In the mouth of two or three witnesses shall every word be established." *(2 Corinthians 13:1)*

"One witness shall not rise up against a man for any iniquity, or for any sin, in any sin that he sinneth: at the mouth of two witnesses, or at the mouth of three witnesses, shall the matter be established." *(Deuteronomy 19:15)*

"But if he will not hear thee, then take with thee one or two more, that in the mouth of two or three witnesses every word may be established."
(Matthew 18:16)

During the Melchizedek's Priesthood

(Abraham, 430 years before the Levitical Priesthood)

"And Melchizedek king of Salem brought forth bread and wine: and he was the priest of the most high God. And he blessed him, and said, Blessed be Abram of the most high God, possessor of heaven and earth: And blessed be the most high God, which hath delivered thine enemies into thy hand. And he gave him tithes of all." *(Genesis 14:18-20)*

See additional references. Genesis 28:18-22; Psalms 110:4; Hebrews 6:20 (eternal), 7:1-11, 7:9 (Levi - Jacob's child), 7:10 (Loins - unborn children of Israel - Genesis 29:34,35)

During the Levitical Priesthood

(Command given to Moses for the Israelites)

"Notwithstanding no devoted thing, that a man shall devote unto the Lord of all that he hath, both of man and beast, and of the field of his possession, shall be sold or redeemed: every devoted thing is most holy unto the Lord. None devoted, which shall be devoted of men, shall be redeemed; but shall surely be put to death. And all the tithe of the land, whether of the seed of the land, or of the fruit of the tree, is the Lord's: it is holy unto the Lord. And if a man will at all redeem ought of his tithes, he shall add thereto the fifth part thereof. And concerning the tithe of the herd, or of the flock, even of whatsoever passeth under the rod, the <u>tenth</u> shall be holy unto the Lord. He shall not search whether it be good or bad, <u>neither shall he change it</u>: and if he change it at all, then both it and the change thereof shall be holy; it shall not be redeemed." *(Leviticus 27:28-33)*

See additional references.   Numbers 18:6-9,20-24 (ordinance forever); Deuteronomy 12:6-7, 12:17-19, 14:22-29,16:16-17, 26:12-15; Proverbs 3:9; Malachi 3:10

Jesus' earthly ministry & after the Levitical Priesthood

Jesus' position on Tithing.

"Think not that I am come to destroy the law, or the prophets: I am not come to destroy, but to fulfil. For verily I say unto you, Till heaven and earth pass, one jot or one tittle shall in no wise pass from the law, till all be fulfilled. Whosoever therefore shall break one of these least commandments, and shall teach men so, he shall be called the least in the kingdom of heaven: but whosoever shall do and teach them, the same shall be called great in the kingdom of heaven." *(Matthew 5:17-19)*

Jesus received financial support for His ministry.

"And it came to pass afterward, that he went throughout every city and village, preaching and shewing the glad tidings of the kingdom of God: and the twelve were with him, And certain women, which had been healed of evil spirits and infirmities, Mary called Magdalene, out of whom went seven devils, And Joanna the wife of Chuza Herod's steward, and Susanna, and many others, <u>which ministered unto him of their substance</u>." *(Luke 8:1-3)*

See additional references. Matthew 5:20, 6:1-4, 10:10,22:2,<u>23:23</u>; Luke 11:42, 16:16,17, 18:11-12; Leviticus 27:30; Isaiah 42:41; Romans 2:12-16; <u>4:11</u>; Galatians <u>3:29</u>; James 2:10,12; Hebrews <u>7:5,9,10</u>; John <u>6:5-13</u>; 2 Corinthians 9:12-14; Romans 2:22 (sacrilege).

Christ words to the hypocrites on tithes

"Woe unto you, scribes and Pharisees, hypocrites! for ye pay tithe of mint and anise and cummin, and have omitted the weightier matters of the law, judgment, mercy, and faith: these ought ye to have done, and not to leave the other undone."
(Matthew 23:23)   Ought (Necessary as binding).

See additional references. Luke 11:42,18:12

The early church gave more than 10%

"And the multitude of them that believed were of one heart and of one soul: neither said any of them that ought of the things which he possessed was his own; but they had all things common. Neither was there any among them that lacked: for as many as were possessors of lands or houses sold them, and brought the prices of the things that were sold, And laid them down at the apostles' feet: and distribution was made unto every man according as he had need. And Joses, who by the apostles was sur-named Barnabas, (which is, being interpreted, The son of consolation,) a Levite, and of the country of Cyprus, Having land, sold it, and brought the money, and laid it at the apostles' feet."
(Acts 4:32,34-37)

Paul said Christians are to walk in Abraham's type faith (Romans 4:12) and are encouraged to excel above 10% (2 Corinthians 8:4,7).

See additional references. 1 Corinthians 9:7-14 (Even so), 16:1-2 (Laying by, in store, prospered, Malachi 3:10); 2 Corinthians 8:1-15; Galatians 6:6; 1 Timothy 5:17-18; Hebrews Chapter 7

The writer of the Hebrews letter taught the ministry of tithing

The death of Christ ended the Leviticus priesthood for administering tithing. This resulted in restoring this function back to the office of the Melchizedek priesthood in Christ Himself (Hebrews 7:11-12). The law was changed not done away with. The system of tithing remains, the administration (spiritual) is different (2 Corinthians 3:3; Hebrews 4:14, 8:1-2, 7:5,8, 11:12-16). This priesthood of Christ is eternal and is to be supported by the children of Abraham (Romans 4:12,16; Hebrews 5:6, 6:20, 7:1-11,17-21, 8:6; Psalms 110:4).

Take your offerings and tithes to the designated place of worship God selects for you.

"But unto the place which the Lord your God shall choose out of all your tribes to put his name there, even unto his habitation shall ye seek, and thither thou shalt come: But when ye go over Jordan, and dwell in the land which the Lord your God giveth you to inherit, and when he giveth you rest from all your enemies round about, so that ye dwell in safety; Then there shall be a place which the Lord your God shall choose to cause his name to dwell there; thither shall ye bring all that I command you; your burnt offerings, and your sacrifices, your tithes, and the heave offering of your hand, and all your choice vows which ye vow unto the Lord." *(Deut. 12:5,10,11)*

HELP SUPPORT GOD'S WORK

Not @ every place you see

"Take heed to thyself that thou offer not thy burnt offerings in every place that thou seest: But in the place which the Lord shall choose in one of thy tribes, there thou shalt offer thy burnt offerings, and there thou shalt do all that I command thee." *(Deuteronomy 12:13,14)*   See. Psalms 132:1-5

See additional references. 1 Kings 9:1-3; 2 Kings 22:1-5 (Doers of the Work); 2 Chronicles 7:12; Jeremiah 23:4; Other ways of support (Deuteronomy 14:24-26; Matthew 21:12-13)

New Testament Greek word for offering

Doron or do'-ron Strong's 1435. It means to give a present, gift or a sacrifice to God. See references. Luke 21:4; Acts 21:26,24:17

New Testament Greek words for tithe

Apodekatoo or ap-od-ek-at-o'-o Strong's 586. Dekatoo or dek-at-o'-o strong's 1183. This word tithe means to pay a tenth of all your increases to God. See references. Matthew 23:23; Luke 11:42,18:12; Hebrews 7:5-9

Remember, as a believer, you are responsible for bringing life to the lost by supporting God's work (Psalms 82:3-5; Proverbs 10:16).

CHAPTER 5

Principle #5

PROVIDE FOR SELF & FAMILY

For self: 2 Thessalonians 3:10

God's confidence in Abraham providing for his family

"For I know him, that he will command his children and his household after him, and they shall keep the way of the Lord, to do justice and judgment; that the Lord may bring upon Abraham that which he hath spoken of him." *(Genesis 18:19)*

Children rights

"Then it shall be, when he maketh his sons to inherit that which he hath, that he may not make the son of the beloved firstborn before the son of the hated, which is indeed the firstborn: But he shall acknowledge the son of the hated for the firstborn, by giving him a double portion of all that he hath: for he is the beginning of his strength; the right of the firstborn is his." *(Deuteronomy 21:16-17)*

PROVIDE FOR SELF & FAMILY

In your will

"A good man leaveth an inheritance to his children's children: and the wealth of the sinner is laid up for the just." *(Proverbs 13:22)* To perpetuate the gospel.

See wisdom.   Psalms 49:10; Proverbs 8:18,21, 17:2; Ecclesiastes 7:11,12; 1 Chronicles 22:5,14-19, 28:7-8

Not all @ once - Receiving or Leaving

"An inheritance may be gotten hastily at the beginning; but the end thereof shall not be blessed."
(Proverbs 20:21)

Read the story of the Prodigal son (Luke 15:11-19). He insisted that his father give him all his inheritance at one time. When he got his wish, he wasted it all on riotous living. Prosperity in the hands of a fool will ultimately destroy him (Deuteronomy 32:5-6; Proverbs 1:32, 3:3,5).

Jesus' teaching of the parable
of the unjust steward

"He that is faithful in that which is least is faithful also in much: and he that is unjust in the least is unjust also in much. If therefore ye have not been faithful in the unrighteous mammon, who will commit to your trust the true riches? And if ye have not been faithful in that which is another man's, who shall give you that which is your own?" *(Luke 16:10-12)*

"Train up a child in the way he should go: and when he is old, he will not depart from it." *(Proverbs 22:6)*

"Behold, the third time I am ready to come to you; and I will not be burdensome to you: for I seek not yours, but you: for the children ought not to lay up for the parents, but the parents for the children." *(2 Corinthians 12:14)*

Provide for their necessities in life

Children - repay your parents or guardians

"But if any widow have children or nephews, let them learn first to shew piety at home, and to requite their parents: for that is good and acceptable before God." *(1 Timothy 5:4)*

"But if any provide not for his own, and specially for those of his own house, he hath denied the faith, and is worse than an infidel." *(1 Timothy 5:8)*

Don't spoil them

"He that spareth his rod hateth his son: but he that loveth him chasteneth him betimes." *(Proverbs 13:24)*

"Chasten thy son while there is hope, and let not thy soul spare for his crying." *(Proverbs 19:18)*

"Foolishness is bound in the heart of a child; but the rod of correction shall drive it far from him." *(Proverbs 22:15)*

"Withhold not correction from the child: for if thou beatest him with the rod, he shall not die. Thou shalt beat him with the rod, and shalt deliver his soul from hell." *(Proverbs 23:13-14)*

"The rod and reproof give wisdom: but a child left to himself bringeth his mother to shame." *(Proverbs 29:15)*

See additional references. 1 Timothy 5:9, 6:8

Don't forget your spiritual family

Acts 2:41-45, 4:31-35, 11:29; Galatians 6:10; 1 John 3:17; Romans 15:25-26

CHAPTER 6
Principle #6
INVEST & SAVE

In Genesis chapter forty one (41), read God's counsel to Joseph about saving.

Words of Solomon about saving

"There is treasure to be desired and oil in the dwelling of the wise; but a foolish man spendeth it up." *(Proverbs 21:20)*

"Go to the ant, thou sluggard; consider her ways, and be wise: Which having no guide, overseer, or ruler, Provideth her meat in the summer, and gathereth her food in the harvest." *(Proverbs 6:6-8)*

"There be four things which are little upon the earth, but they are exceeding wise: The ants are a people not strong, yet they prepare their meat in the summer." *(Proverbs 30:24-25)*

Do not try to save all you earn. Your focus should not be on the accumulation of earthly wealth - but on the proper distribution of it (Luke 12:15-21).

Investment Income

This type of income is money gained from participating in an activity where money is placed at risk - except for the kingdom of God (Genesis 8:21-22) - for the purpose of making an honest financial profit.

The Investment Process !

• <u>God supplies the seed (money)</u>. 2 Corinthians 9:10; Hosea 2:8; John 3:27.   Only - if you are a sower.

• <u>You prepare the soil/ground</u>. Isaiah 28:24-26 AMP; Deut. 14:5; Jer. 4:3; Hosea 10:12; Proverbs 28:19

• <u>You sow (invest/plant) the seed</u>.   Psalms 126:5-6; Luke 6:38; 2 Corinthians 9:6; Gal. 6:7; Heb. 4:2; Leviticus 27:30; Malachi 3:10-11; John 12:24

   Only sow your seed in good soil. Isaiah 32:20 AMP; Ecclesiastes 11:1; Matthew 13:23

• <u>You water (nurture) the seed</u>. Ecclesiastes 11:4,6; Proverbs 18:20-21; Malachi 3:13-14; 1 Corinthians 3:5-8; Galatians 6:9; Hebrews 4:2; Proverbs 12:14 Thank God - for the increase.   Psalms 147:7-8; Deuteronomy 26:10-15; Isaiah 55:10; Hosea 10:12

• <u>Protect the seed</u>. Lev. 26:15-16; Deut. 28:15,33,38, 51; Prov. 18:21; Mal. 3:13-14;Micah 6:15; Jer. 12:13

• <u>God multiplies (increases) the seed</u>. Genesis 8:22; 2 Chron. 26:1,5; Jer. 5:24; 1 Cor. 3:6; Hosea 2:8; Lev. 26:3-5;2 Cor. 9:10;Gen. 26:12;Psalms 126:5-6

• <u>Honor God</u>.   Lev. 27:30; Deut. 36:2; Prov. 3:9 AMP; Mal. 3:10; Matt. 23:23; 1 Cor. 16:2; Psalms 147:7-8

Let's look at receiving investment income from the following six (6) biblical investment considerations.

1) Why should I invest ?

- To obey the command of God. Matthew 25:27; Luke 19:11-26 (Parable of the pounds)
- To provide for family needs. 1 Timothy 5:8
- To be able to give more. Luke 12:48,19:12-26
- To promote the saving gospel. Proverbs 10:16; Romans 10:9-17; Philippians 4:16; Rev. 21:7-8
- To promote the transforming gospel. 1 Tim. 1:4; Romans 12:2;2 Timothy 3:16-17;Ephesians 4:11-15
- To overcome future calamities. Genesis 41:29-35
- To leave an inheritance. Proverbs 13:22, 19:14, 21:20, 30:24-25; Ecclesiastes 7:11; 2 Cor. 12:14

2) When should I invest ?

- Now. Don't wait for all conditions to be favorable. There will always be an element of risk outside the kingdom of God. See reference Ecclesiastes 11:4. You can't control the risk. However, you can mini-mize it by doing your home work (Proverbs 24:27). If you fail, try again (Psalms 37:23-24;Prov. 24:16).

3) Where should I invest ?

• The kingdom of God. This represents God's true Christian ministries. There is always an opportunity to invest and to receive a sure return. Genesis 8:22; Zechariah 8:12;Matthew 9:37-38;2 Corinthians 8:4. The greatest investment you can ever make is into the kingdom of God. See Malachi 3:10-12 (unlimited return); Prov. 8:19 AMP,11:30,19:17; Matt. 6:19-21,33,19:29;Luke 6:38;Psalms 126:6;Galatians 6:9.

Why You Should Invest Into The Kingdom of God

(A) There is no greater investment than honoring God by contributing to the salvation and the transformation of souls. This type of investment is known as a spiritual investment. **(B)** This investment yields eternal rewards (Philippians 4:17; 1 Peter 1:3-4; Revelation 22:12; Matthew 6:20; 1 Timothy 6:19). **(C)** It also yields earthly rewards (Proverbs 11:31). All non-spiritual investments are only temporal or temporary (2 Corinthians 4:18).

• Other places of financial investments. Savings; Gold; Mutual Funds; Stocks; Real Estate; Your business; Other business owners; Life Insurance; IRAs; College Planning; Charitable Gift Annuity; US Treasury Bonds; US Treasury TIPS; and Witty (practical) Godly ideas (Proverbs 8:12).

See the story of the parable of talents - Matt. 25:14-30.

4) How should I invest ?

- Make God your senior partner. Proverbs 3:5-6
- Seek Godly counsel. Psalms 32:8,33:11,37:23; 119:24;Prov. 12:15;Lev. 19:31;Isaiah 9:6;Heb. 4:12; Prov. 11:14,15:22,19:20-21;2 Samuel 22:31,33; Job 37:16; Deut. 29:9; Eccl. 12:13; Isaiah 46:10, 48:17; Joshua 1:8
- Be led by the Spirit. John 16:13; 1 Cor. 2:9-11
- Avoid unwise investments. Ecclesiastes 5:13-14; Proverbs 24:27, 29:24 (avoid the thief); Rev. 3:18
- Diversify Wisely. Eccl. 11:2; Lev. 19:19; Deut. 22:9

5) How much should I invest ?
- Not everything. Luke 12:16-21,34
- Establish a budget. Luke 14:28-30; John 6:1-12
- General rule. Between 5 &10% (outside the kingdom)

6) How long should I wait ?
Learn to be patient and consistent

(consistently invest, even if only a little - at a time)

"Dishonest money dwindles away, but he who gathers money little by little makes it grow."
(Proverbs 13:11 NIV)

"The thoughts of the diligent tend only to plenteousness; but of every one that is hasty only to want."
(Proverbs 21:5)

INVEST & SAVE

In Proverbs 19:2 (AMP), King Solomon said: When you disregard knowledge, get in a hurry, this will cause you to sin and miss the mark.

"And let us not be weary in well doing: for in due season we shall reap, if we faint not." *(Galatians 6:9)*

Learn to be patient, prayerful and praiseful

"Be careful for nothing; but in every thing by prayer and supplication with thanksgiving let your requests be made known unto God." *(Philippians 4:6)*

Remember to seek Christian professionals - such as financial advisors, investors, trust and estate planning attorneys, accountants, tax consultants and other industry related professionals. See references Psalms 1:1, Psalms 37:30-31 and Proverbs 15:22.

CHAPTER 7

Principle #7

PAY YOUR VOWS

A vow is a binding pledge or promise to honor an agreement between two parties.

God's instruction for making a vow

"If a man vow a vow unto the Lord, or swear an oath to bind his soul with a bond; he shall not break his word, he shall do according to all that proceedeth out of his mouth." *(Numbers 30:2)*

Elisha and the widow woman

"Now there cried a certain woman of the wives of the sons of the prophets unto Elisha, saying, Thy servant my husband is dead; and thou knowest that thy servant did fear the Lord: and the creditor is come to take unto him my two sons to be bondmen. And Elisha said unto her, What shall I do for thee? tell me, what hast thou in the house? And she said, Thine handmaid hath not any thing in the house, save a pot of oil. Then he said, Go, borrow thee vessels abroad of all thy neighbours, even empty vessels; borrow not a few. And when thou art come in, thou shalt shut the door upon thee and upon thy sons, and shalt pour out into all those vessels, and thou shalt set aside that which is full. So she went from him, and shut the door upon her and upon her sons, who brought the vessels to her; and she poured out. And it came to pass, when the vessels were full, that she said unto her son, Bring me yet a vessel. And he said unto her, There is not a vessel more. And the oil stayed. Then she came and told the man of God. And he said, Go, sell the oil, and pay thy debt, and live thou and thy children of the rest." *(2 Kings 4:1-7)*

"The wicked borroweth, and payeth not again: but the righteous sheweth mercy, and giveth." *(Psalms 37:21)*

"Vow, and pay unto the Lord your God: let all that be round about him bring presents unto him that ought to be feared." *(Psalms 76:11)*

"I will pay my vows unto the Lord now in the presence of all his people." *(Psalms 116:14)*

Give praises to God to uphold (Psalms 61:8).

WHAT TO-DO WITH MONEY

Especially to God

"When thou vowest a vow unto God, defer not to pay it; for he hath no pleasure in fools: pay that which thou hast vowed.   Better is it that thou shouldest not vow, than that thou shouldest vow and not pay." *(Ecclesiastes 5:4-5)*

Jacob's vow of tithe @ Bethel

"And Jacob vowed a vow, saying, If God will be with me, and will keep me in this way that I go, and will give me bread to eat, and raiment to put on,   So that I come again to my father's house in peace; then shall the Lord be my God: And this stone, which I have set for a pillar, shall be God's house: and of all that thou shalt give me I will surely give the tenth unto thee." *(Genesis 28:20-22)*

The tithe belongs to God. Leviticus 27:30; Malachi 3:7,8

Vow of offering

Psalms 76:11; Malachi 3:3; 2 Corinthians 9:6-7; Luke 19:1-10

"Owe no man any thing, but to love one another: for he that loveth another hath fulfilled the law." *(Romans 13:8)*   See. Romans 12:17; 1 Timothy 2:2

PAY YOUR VOWS

"Agree with thine adversary quickly, whiles thou art in the way with him; lest at any time the adversary deliver thee to the judge, and the judge deliver thee to the officer, and thou be cast into prison. Verily I say unto thee, Thou shalt by no means come out thence, till thou hast paid the uttermost farthing." *(Matthew 5:25-26)*

Jesus paid His bills

"Notwithstanding, lest we should offend them, go thou to the sea, and cast an hook, and take up the fish that first cometh up; and when thou hast opened his mouth, thou shalt find a piece of money: that take, and give unto them for me and thee." *(Matthew 17:27)*

Words of Paul

"Give everyone what you owe him: If you owe taxes, pay taxes; if revenue, then revenue; if respect, then respect; if honor, then honor." *(Romans 13:7 NIV)*

Pay your vows on time, protect your credit and stay in good standing with man and God.

See additional references. 1 Samuel 1:21; Nehemiah 10:32-39 (especially to the house of God); Psalms 22:25,66:13-14; Proverbs 3:27-28, 22:7; Malachi 3:7-9; Mark 12:17; Galatians 6:10

CHAPTER 8

Principle #8

TEACH YOUR CHILDREN FINANCIAL STEWARDSHIP

<u>That they might be a good steward, live in the true blessings of God, teach their children and give proper accountability</u>

God's instructions to the children of Israel

"Only take heed to thyself, and keep thy soul diligently, lest thou forget the things which thine eyes have seen, and lest they depart from thy heart all the days of thy life: but teach them thy sons, and thy sons' sons; Specially the day that thou stoodest before the Lord thy God in Horeb, when the Lord said unto me, Gather me the people together, and I will make them <u>hear my words</u>, that they may learn to fear me all the days that they shall live upon the earth, and that they may teach their children." *(Deuteronomy. 4:9-10)*

"That the generation to come might know them, even the children which should be born; who should arise and declare them to their children: That they might set their hope in God, and not forget the works of God, but keep his commandments: And might not be as their fathers, a stubborn and rebellious generation; a generation that set not their heart aright, and whose spirit was not stedfast with God."
(Psalms 78:6-8)

They must hear the word of God. Romans 10:17

"Train up a child in the way he should go: and when he is old, he will not depart from it."
(Proverbs 22:6)

Remember, God's way is the right way (Psalms 1:6; Isaiah 48:17).

God's confidence &
blessing plan
through Abraham

"For I know him, that he will command his children and his household after him, and they shall keep the way of the Lord, to do justice and judgment; that the Lord may bring upon Abraham that which he hath spoken of him." *(Genesis 18:19)*

WHAT TO-DO WITH MONEY

Abraham - father of all who believe

"And he received the sign of circumcision, a seal of the righteousness of the faith which he had yet being uncircumcised: that he might be the father of all them that believe, though they be not circumcised; that righteousness might be imputed unto them also." *(Romans 4:11)*

Abraham's spiritual seed & heirs by promise

"And if ye be Christ's, then are ye Abraham's seed, and heirs according to the promise."
(Galatians 3:29)   The Promise. Genesis 12:1-3

How to receive the promise. Hebrews 10:35-36

Charge of David to his son Solomon

"Now the days of David drew nigh that he should die; and he charged Solomon his son, saying, I go the way of all the earth: be thou strong therefore, and shew thyself a man; And keep the charge of the Lord thy God, to walk in his ways, to keep his statutes, and his commandments, and his judgments, and his testimonies, as it is written in the law of Moses, that thou mayest prosper in all that thou doest, and whithersoever thou turnest thyself: That the Lord may continue his word which he spake con-

cerning me, saying, If thy children take heed to their way, to walk before me in truth with all their heart and with all their soul, there shall not fail thee (said he) a man on the throne of Israel."
(1 Kings 2:1-4)

"Now, my son, the Lord be with thee; and prosper thou, and build the house of the Lord thy God, as he hath said of thee. Only the Lord give thee wisdom and understanding, and give thee charge concerning Israel, that thou mayest keep the law of the Lord thy God. Then shalt thou prosper, if thou takest heed to fulfil the statutes and judgments which the Lord charged Moses with concerning Israel: be strong, and of good courage; dread not, nor be dismayed." *(1 Chronicles 22:11-13)*

"Now these are the commandments, the statutes, and the judgments, which the Lord your God commanded to teach you, that ye might do them in the land whither ye go to possess it: That thou mightest fear the Lord thy God, to keep all his statutes and his commandments, which I command thee, thou, and thy son, and thy son's son, all the days of thy life; and that thy days may be prolonged. Hear therefore, O Israel, and observe to do it; that it may be well with thee, and that ye may increase mightily, as the Lord God of thy fathers hath promised thee, in the land that floweth with milk and honey. Hear, O Israel: The Lord our God is one Lord: And thou shalt love the Lord thy God with all thine heart, and with all thy soul, and with all thy might. And these words, which I command thee this day, shall be in thine heart: And thou shalt teach them diligently unto thy children, and shalt talk of them when thou sittest in thine house, and when thou walkest by the way, and when thou liest down, and when thou risest up. And when thy son asketh thee in time to come, saying, What mean the testimonies, and the statutes, and the judgments, which the Lord our God hath commanded you?" *(Deuteronomy 6:1-7,20)*

"A wise son heareth his father's instruction: but a scorner heareth not rebuke." *(Proverbs 13:1)*

"Children, obey your parents in the Lord: for this is right. Honour thy father and mother; (which is the first commandment with promise;) That it may be well with thee, and thou mayest live long on the earth. And, ye fathers, provoke not your children to wrath: but bring them up in the nurture and admonition of the Lord." *(Ephesians 6:1-4)*

See additional references. Deuteronomy 11:18-21, 31:12-13; Proverbs 1:7,8,9, 4:1, 5:23, 13:18,22, 20:20, 30:17; 1 Samuel 1:21-24, 3:19; Luke 2:51;

Colossians 3:20,21;Titus 3:8-11;Hebrews 12:5,7,11; Psalms 127:1; Proverbs 6:20-22, 8:10,11,18-21, 24:3-4; Ecclesiastes 7:11; Isaiah 59:21

Read Hebrews 13:17 for blessings through submission to delegated authority.

Remember your example
1 Corinthians 11:1; Luke 6:40

**The ultimate goal of teaching your children
is the salvation of their lives -
then the sanctification - transformation of their
souls, which includes teaching them sound
biblical financial stewardship**

"And that from a child thou hast known the holy scriptures, which are able to make thee wise unto salvation through faith which is in Christ Jesus. All scripture is given by inspiration of God, and is profitable for doctrine, for reproof, for correction, for instruction in righteousness: That the man of God may be perfect, thoroughly furnished unto all good works." *(2 Timothy 3:15-17)*

CHAPTER 9

Principle #9

HELP THE LESS FORTUNATE

It is required of you

Old Testament command

"And if thy brother be waxen poor, and fallen in decay with thee; then thou shalt relieve him: yea, though he be a stranger, or a sojourner; that he may live with thee." *(Leviticus 25:35)*

"But who am I, and what is my people, that we should be able to offer so willingly after this sort? for all things come of thee, and of thine own have we given thee." *(1 Chronicles 29:14)*

"Withhold not good from them to whom it is due, when it is in the power of thine hand to do it. Say not unto thy neighbour, Go, and come again, and to morrow I will give; when thou hast it by thee." *(Proverbs 3:27-28)*

"Is it not to deal thy bread to the hungry, and that thou bring the poor that are cast out to thy house? when thou seest the naked, that thou cover him; and that thou hide not thyself from thine own flesh?" *(Isaiah 58:7)*

New Testament command

"But whoso hath this world's good, and seeth his brother have need, and shutteth up his bowels of compassion from him, how dwelleth the love of God in him?" *(1 John 3:17)*

"But he that knew not, and did commit things worthy of stripes, shall be beaten with few stripes. For unto whomsoever much is given, of him shall be much required: and to whom men have committed much, of him they will ask the more." *(Luke 12:48)*

Look at it as a privilege

Especially the rich

"Charge them that are rich in this world, that they be not highminded, nor trust in uncertain riches, but in the living God, who giveth us richly all things to enjoy; That they do good, that they be rich in good works, ready to distribute, willing to communicate." *(1 Timothy 6:17-18)*

Story of the good Samaritan

"And Jesus answering said, A certain man went down from Jerusalem to Jericho, and fell among thieves, which stripped him of his raiment, and wounded him, and departed, leaving him half dead. And by chance there came down a certain priest that way: and when he saw him, he passed by on the other side. And likewise a Levite, when he was at the place, came and looked on him, and passed by on the other side. But a certain Samaritan, as he journeyed, came where he was: and when he saw him, he had compassion on him, And went to him, and bound up his wounds, pouring in oil and wine, and set him on his own beast, and brought him to an inn, and took care of him. And on the morrow when he departed, he took out two pence, and gave them to the host, and said unto him, Take care of him; and whatsoever thou spendest more, when I come again, I will repay thee. Which now of these three, thinkest thou, was neighbour unto him that fell among the thieves? And he said, He that shewed mercy on him. Then said Jesus unto him, Go, and do thou likewise." *(Luke 10:30-37)*

"Praying us with much intreaty that we would receive the gift, and take upon us the fellowship of the ministering to the saints." *(2 Corinthians 8:4)*

"Now he that ministereth seed to the sower both minister bread for your food, and multiply your seed sown, and increase the fruits of your righteousness." *(2 Corinthians 9:10)*

"Let him that stole steal no more: but rather let him labour, working with his hands the thing which is good, that he may have to give to him that needeth." *(Ephesians 4:28)*

"I have shewed you all things, how that so labouring ye ought to support the weak, and to remember the words of the Lord Jesus, how he said, It is more blessed to give than to receive." *(Acts 20:35)*

James said: Faith without works is useless

"If a brother or sister be naked, and destitute of daily food, And one of you say unto them, Depart in peace, be ye warmed and filled; notwithstanding ye give them not those things which are needful to the body; what doth it profit? Even so faith, if it hath not works, is dead, being alone. Yea, a man may say, Thou hast faith, and I have works: shew me thy faith without thy works, and I will shew thee my faith by my works." *(James 2:15-18)*

You must not have a spirit of selfishness

"Whoso stoppeth his ears at the cry of the poor, he also shall cry himself, but shall not be heard." *(Proverbs 21:13)*

"Open thy mouth, judge righteously, and plead the cause of the poor and needy." *(Proverbs 31:9)*

"He that loveth silver shall not be satisfied with silver; nor he that loveth abundance with increase: this is also vanity. There is a sore evil which I have seen under the sun, namely, riches kept for the owners thereof to their hurt." *(Ecclesiastes 5:10,13)*

See other references. Galatians 5:14,6:2; Matthew 25:35-45

A heart of giving can bring you healing !

"Blessed is he that considereth the poor: the Lord will deliver him in time of trouble. The Lord will preserve him, and keep him alive; and he shall be blessed upon the earth: and thou wilt not deliver him unto the will of his enemies. The Lord will strengthen him upon the bed of languishing: thou wilt make all his bed in his sickness." *(Psalms 41:1-3)*

HELP THE LESS FORTUNATE

Giving prevents poverty for others

"He that oppresseth the poor reproacheth his Maker: but he that honoureth him hath mercy on the poor." *(Proverbs 14:31)*

"Whoso mocketh the poor reproacheth his Maker: and he that is glad at calamities shall not be unpunished." *(Proverbs 17:5)*

"Defend the poor and fatherless: do justice to the afflicted and needy. Deliver the poor and needy: rid them out of the hand of the wicked."*(Psalms 82:3-4)*

Giving prevents poverty for yourself

"Whoso stoppeth his ears at the cry of the poor, he also shall cry himself, but shall not be heard." *(Proverbs 21:13)*

"Then shall he say also unto them on the left hand, Depart from me, ye cursed, into everlasting fire, prepared for the devil and his angels: For I was an hungred, and ye gave me no meat: I was thirsty, and ye gave me no drink: I was a stranger, and ye took me not in: naked, and ye clothed me not: sick, and in prison, and ye visited me not. Then shall they also answer him, saying, Lord, when saw we thee an hungred, or athirst, or a stranger, or naked, or sick, or in prison, and did not minister unto thee? Then shall he answer them, saying, Verily I say unto you, Inasmuch as ye did it not to one of the least of these, ye did it not to me. And these shall go away into everlasting punishment: but the righteous into life eternal." *(Matthew 25:41-46)*

"Be not deceived; God is not mocked: for whatsoever a man soweth, that shall he also reap. For he that soweth to his flesh shall of the flesh reap corruption; but he that soweth to the Spirit shall of the Spirit reap life everlasting." *(Galatians 6:7-8)*

Giving allows you to grow in Godly perfection and add fruit to your heavenly account

"Jesus said unto him, If thou wilt be perfect, go and sell that thou hast, and give to the poor, and thou shalt have treasure in heaven: and come and follow me." *(Matthew 19:21)*

An act of brotherly love

"Bear ye one another's burdens, and so fulfil the law of Christ." *(Galatians 6:2)*

Warning:
for not helping the poor and needy

"Hath oppressed the poor and needy, hath spoiled by violence, hath not restored the pledge, and hath lifted up his eyes to the idols, hath committed abomination, Hath given forth upon usury, and hath taken increase: shall he then live? he shall not live: he hath done all these abominations; he shall surely die; his blood shall be upon him." *(Ezekiel 18:12-13)*

"And her prophets have daubed them with untempered morter, seeing vanity, and divining lies unto them, saying, Thus saith the Lord God, when the Lord hath not spoken. The people of the land have used oppression, and exercised robbery, and have vexed the poor and needy: yea, they have oppressed the stranger wrongfully. And I sought for a man among them, that should make up the hedge, and stand in the gap before me for the land, that I should not destroy it: but I found none. Therefore have I poured out mine indignation upon them; I have consumed them with the fire of my wrath: their own way have I recompensed upon their heads, saith the Lord God." *(Ezekiel 22:28-31)*

"He hath dispersed, he hath given to the poor; his righteousness endureth for ever; his horn shall be exalted with honour." *(Psalms 112:9)*

"He that hath pity upon the poor lendeth unto the Lord; and that which he hath given will he pay him again." *(Proverbs 19:17)*

Your return. Matthew 19:29; Proverbs 19:17; 2 Corinthians 9:6; Galatians 6:7-9

"He that giveth unto the poor shall not lack: but he that hideth his eyes shall have many a curse." *(Proverbs 28:27)*

"There is that scattereth, and yet increaseth; and there is that withholdeth more than is meet, but it tendeth to poverty." *(Proverbs 11:24)*

Remember !

"The Lord maketh poor, and maketh rich: he bringeth low, and lifteth up." *(1 Samuel 2:7)*

"He that despiseth his neighbour sinneth: but he that hath mercy on the poor, happy is he." *(Proverbs 14:21)*

HELP THE LESS FORTUNATE

"And if thou draw out thy soul to the hungry, and satisfy the afflicted soul; then shall thy light rise in obscurity, and thy darkness be as the noonday: And the Lord shall guide thee continually, and satisfy thy soul in drought, and make fat thy bones: and thou shalt be like a watered garden, and like a spring of water, whose waters fail not. And they that shall be of thee shall build the old waste places: thou shalt raise up the foundations of many generations; and thou shalt be called, The repairer of the breach, The restorer of paths to dwell in." *(Isaiah 58:10-12)*

See additional references. Matthew 10:42,12:35; Luke 14:13-14,18:18-22; 2 Corinthians 9:6-8; 8:14; Amos 8:4-14; Deuteronomy 15:7,9; Proverbs 22:9

Remember...
a charitable heart will bring you healing !

See references: Psalms 41:1-3; 1 Kings 17:8-24; 1 Corinthians 11:22-30; Acts 9:36-43, 28:1-10

In Psalms 41:1-3, God has promised seven things for those with a charitable heart. (1) Deliverance in time of trouble; (2) Preservation;   (3) Revived life; (4) Blessed upon the earth; (5) Deliverance from enemies; (6) Strength; (7) Recovery in sickness and weakness.

There is always the opportunity to help (Mark 14:7).

CHAPTER 10
Principle #10
WORSHIP GOD

<u>An act of adoration and reverential regard to God</u>

You worship the true God - Elohim, Jehovah, through your giving to the kingdom's work. This acknowledges God's Lordship in your life. The Old Testament saints worshiped God through their giving.

Past

The children of Israel

"And they came, every one whose heart stirred him up, and every one whom his spirit made willing, and they brought the Lord's offering to the work of the tabernacle of the congregation, and for all his service, and for the holy garments. And they came, both men and women, as many as were willing hearted, and brought bracelets, and earrings, and rings, and tablets, all jewels of gold: and every man that offered offered an offering of gold unto the Lord. And every man, with whom was found blue, and purple, and scarlet, and fine linen, and goats' hair, and red skins of rams, and badgers' skins, brought them. Every one that did offer an offering of silver and brass brought the Lord's offering: and every man, with whom was found shittim wood for any work of the service, brought it. And all the women that were wise hearted did spin with their hands, and brought that which they had spun, both of blue, and of purple, and of scarlet, and of fine linen. And all the women whose heart stirred them up in wisdom spun goats' hair. And the rulers brought onyx stones, and stones to be set, for the ephod, and for the breastplate; And spice, and oil for the light, and for the anointing oil, and for the sweet incense. The children of Israel brought a willing offering unto the Lord, every man and woman, whose heart made them willing to bring for all manner of work, which the Lord had commanded to be made by the hand of Moses." *(Exodus 35:21-29)*

Worshipping God through giving commemorates (reminds) you of His mercy toward you - and acknowledges His presence.

"And thou shalt speak and say before the Lord thy God, A Syrian ready to perish was my father, and he went down into Egypt, and sojourned there with a few, and became there a nation, great, mighty, and populous: And the Egyptians evil entreated us, and

afflicted us, and laid upon us hard bondage: And when we cried unto the Lord God of our fathers, the Lord heard our voice, and looked on our affliction, and our labour, and our oppression: And the Lord brought us forth out of Egypt with a mighty hand, and with an outstretched arm, and with great terribleness, and with signs, and with wonders: And he hath brought us into this place, and hath given us this land, even a land that floweth with milk and honey. <u>And now, behold, I have brought the first-fruits of the land, which thou, O Lord, hast given me. And thou shalt set it before the Lord thy God, and worship before the Lord thy God</u>:"
(Deuteronomy 26:5-10)

In 1 Chronicles 28:2, 29:1-20 and Matthew 2:11, you will see that worship and giving go together.

Whatever you worship - will eventually control you. Psalms 135:15-18

Administering spiritual gifts - edifies (builds up) the body of Christ

See these references. Romans 12:3-8,13;
1 Corinthians 12:4-11; 2 Corinthians 8:1-5, 9:11-13;
1 Peter 4:10

Only God is to be worshiped

"For thou shalt worship no other god: for the Lord, whose name is Jealous, is a jealous God." (*Exodus 34:14*)

See additional references. Isaiah 2:8; Revelation 19:10,22:8-9

Sanctuary service

In the Old Testament, the primary way of entering into God's presence was worshipping Him through the offering of sacrifices.

Sin offerings were for moral offenses. The Thank you offerings were the expressing of one's gratitude for God's goodness and fellowship.

In the New Testament, the sin offering was done away with, by the death of Christ (Hebrews 9:11-14,10:1-14).

However, the thanks offering is still accepted of God (1 Thessalonians 5:16,18; Ephesians 5:19-20; Philippians 4:18; Colossians 3:15,17; Hebrews 13:15-16).

Past

See additional references. Genesis 14:18-20;
Exodus 35:21-29; Deuteronomy 14:22-29;
1 Chronicles 16:29, 29:2-20; Matthew 2:2,7-11,4:9-10;
Psalms 35:18, 95:2-3, 96:7-9,116:17;
Numbers 28:1-2; 2 Chronicles 29:3,7-36

Wise men offered gifts in the worship of the Messiah

"When they had heard the king, they departed; and, lo, the star, which they saw in the east, went before them, till it came and stood over where the young child was. When they saw the star, they rejoiced with exceeding great joy. And when they were come into the house, they saw the young child with Mary his mother, and fell down, and worshipped him: and when they had opened their treasures, they presented unto him gifts; gold, and frankincense, and myrrh." *(Matthew 2:9-11)*

Vain giving prohibits true worship

"Hear the word of the Lord, ye rulers of Sodom; give ear unto the law of our God, ye people of Gomorrah. To what purpose is the multitude of your sacrifices unto me? saith the Lord: I am full of the burnt offerings of rams, and the fat of fed beasts; and I delight not in the blood of bullocks, or of lambs, or of he goats. When ye come to appear before me, who hath required this at your hand, to tread my courts? Bring no more vain oblations; incense is an abomination unto me; the new moons and sabbaths, the calling of assemblies, I cannot away with; it is iniquity, even the solemn meeting. Your new moons and your appointed feasts my soul hateth: they are a trouble unto me; I am weary to bear them. And when ye spread forth your hands, I will hide mine eyes from you: yea, when ye make many prayers, I will not hear: your hands are full of blood. Wash you, make you clean; put away the evil of your doings from before mine eyes; cease to do evil; Learn to do well; seek judgment, relieve the oppressed, judge the fatherless, plead for the widow. Come now, and let us reason together, saith the Lord: though your sins be as scarlet, they shall be as white as snow; though they be red like crimson, they shall be as wool. If ye be willing and obedient, ye shall eat the good of the land: But if ye refuse and rebel, ye shall be devoured with the sword: for the mouth of the Lord hath spoken it." *(Isaiah 1:10-20)*

See additional reference. Malachi 1:7-14

WHAT TO-DO WITH MONEY

God abandoned His presence in the tabernacle at Shiloh until His sanctuary services were reinstated. The sinful lifestyles of the people prohibited true worship. See additional references. Jeremiah 7:1-11; Psalms 78:58-72

Past - Present

"And he looked up, and saw the rich men casting their gifts into the treasury. And he saw also a certain poor widow casting in thither two mites. And he said, Of a truth I say unto you, that this poor widow hath cast in more than they all: For all these have of their abundance cast in unto the offerings of God: but she of her penury hath cast in all the living that she had." *(Luke 21:1-4)*

We now offer our gifts (Ecclesiastes 7:11-12; Hebrews 13:16) and our bodies (Romans 12:1) a living sacrifice to God through our High Priest Jesus (Hebrews 7:8), who then blesses (John 6:5-13) them and offers the complete sacrifice to God as a sweet smelling savor (Philippians 4:14-18). This is true worship. Praise be to God for the breakthrough.

See additional references. 1 Corinthians 16:2; Acts 20:7; Mark 11:17; Luke 19:46

Read the book of Hebrews Chapter seven and ten for revelation on natural and spiritual worship.

Future Millennium

"And it shall come to pass in the last days, that the mountain of the Lord's house shall be established in the top of the mountains, and shall be exalted above the hills; and all nations shall flow unto it."
(Isaiah 2:2)

The Ethiopian

"In that time shall the present be brought unto the Lord of hosts of a people scattered and peeled, and from a people terrible from their beginning hitherto; a nation meted out and trodden under foot, whose land the rivers have spoiled, to the place of the name of the Lord of hosts, the mount Zion."
(Isaiah 18:7)

"Even them will I bring to my holy mountain, and make them joyful in my house of prayer: their burnt offerings and their sacrifices shall be accepted upon mine altar; for mine house shall be called an house of prayer for all people." *(Isaiah 56:7)*

WHAT TO-DO WITH MONEY

Future fellowship at the Temple in Jerusalem

"And it shall come to pass in the last days, that the mountain of the Lord's house shall be established in the top of the mountains, and shall be exalted above the hills; and all nations shall flow unto it. And many people shall go and say, Come ye, and let us go up to the mountain of the Lord, to the house of the God of Jacob; and he will teach us of his ways, and we will walk in his paths: for out of Zion shall go forth the law, and the word of the Lord from Jerusalem. And he shall judge among the nations, and shall rebuke many people: and they shall beat their swords into plowshares, and their spears into pruninghooks: nation shall not lift up sword against nation, neither shall they learn war any more." *(Isaiah 2:2-4)*

"And it shall come to pass, that every one that is left of all the nations which came against Jerusalem shall even go up from year to year to worship the King, the Lord of hosts, and to keep the feast of tabernacles. And it shall be, that whoso will not come up of all the families of the earth unto Jerusalem to worship the King, the Lord of hosts, even upon them shall be no rain. And if the family of Egypt go not up, and come not, that have no rain;

there shall be the plague, wherewith the Lord will smite the heathen that come not up to keep the feast of tabernacles. This shall be the punishment of Egypt, and the punishment of all nations that come not up to keep the feast of tabernacles. In that day shall there be upon the bells of the horses, HOLINESS UNTO THE LORD; and the pots in the Lord's house shall be like the bowls before the altar. Yea, every pot in Jerusalem and in Judah shall be holiness unto the Lord of hosts: and all they that sacrifice shall come and take of them, and seethe therein: and in that day there shall be no more the Canaanite in the house of the Lord of hosts."
(Zechariah 14:16-21)

See additional references. Ezekiel 45:17 and chapter 46

Future new earth

"For as the new heavens and the new earth, which I will make, shall remain before me, saith the Lord, so shall your seed and your name remain. And it shall come to pass, that from one new moon to another, and from one sabbath to another, shall all flesh come to worship before me, saith the Lord."
(Isaiah 66:22-23)

Future Eternal Temple
Where Christ will reign

"Because of thy temple at Jerusalem shall kings <u>bring</u> <u>presents</u> unto thee. Rebuke the company of spearmen, the multitude of the bulls, with the calves of the people, <u>till every one submit himself with pieces of silver</u>: scatter thou the people that delight in war. Princes shall come out of Egypt; Ethiopia shall soon stretch out her hands unto God. Sing unto God, ye kingdoms of the earth; O sing praises unto the Lord; Selah:" *(Psalms 68:29-32)*

God is even now restoring the tabernacle of David. Isaiah 9:6-7,16:5; Jeremiah 30:9; Ezekiel 34:23,24,37:24-25; Hosea 3:4-5; Acts 15:13-18

All will one day bow & worship
the King of Kings with gifts

"They that dwell in the wilderness shall bow before him; and his enemies shall lick the dust. The kings of Tarshish and of the isles shall <u>bring</u> <u>presents</u>: the kings of Sheba and Seba shall <u>offer</u> <u>gifts</u>. Yea, all kings shall fall down before him: all nations shall serve him. For he shall deliver the needy when he crieth; the poor also, and him that hath no helper. He shall spare the poor and needy, and shall save the souls of the needy. He shall redeem their soul from deceit and violence: and precious shall their blood be in his sight. And he shall live, and to him shall be given of the gold of Sheba: prayer also shall be made for him continually; and daily shall he be praised. There shall be an handful of corn in the earth upon the top of the mountains; the fruit there-of shall shake like Lebanon: and they of the city shall flourish like grass of the earth. His name shall endure for ever: his name shall be continued as long as the sun: and men shall be blessed in him: all nations shall call him blessed. Blessed be the Lord God, the God of Israel, who only doeth wondrous things. And blessed be his glorious name for ever: and let the whole earth be filled with his glory; Amen, and Amen. The prayers of David the son of Jesse are ended." *(Psalms 72:9-20)*

"Vow, and pay unto the Lord your God: let all that be round about him bring presents unto him that ought to be feared." *(Psalms 76:11)*

 All the earth will bow and worship the one true God, even the rich. See Psalms 22:27-29

Satan's ultimate goal is to get you to worship him - by any means necessary. You must learn to resist him as Jesus did.   See reference. Matthew 4:1-11

CHAPTER 11

Principle #11

EXERCISE OBEDIENCE TO YOUR SPIRITUAL GIFT

The gift of giving

This is a motivational gift - given by the Father. Therefore, those that have this gift should gladly exercise it. Those who operate in this gift, love to give (contribute) to help others and advance the kingdom's work. They are self-motivated, and are excellent examples for all.

a gift for helping others

"For I say, through the grace given unto me, to every man that is among you, not to think of himself more highly than he ought to think; but to think soberly, according as God hath dealt to every man the measure of faith. For as we have many members in one

body, and all members have not the same office: So we, being many, are one body in Christ, and every one members one of another. Having then gifts differing according to the grace that is given to us, whether prophecy, let us prophesy according to the proportion of faith; Or ministry, let us wait on our ministering: or he that teacheth, on teaching; Or he that exhorteth, on exhortation: he that giveth, let him do it with simplicity; he that ruleth, with diligence; he that sheweth mercy, with cheerfulness. Distributing to the necessity of saints; given to hospitality."
(Romans 12:3-8,13)

Paul's confidence of this gift of the churches of Macedonia

"Moreover, brethren, we do you to wit of the grace of God bestowed on the churches of Macedonia; How that in a great trial of affliction the abundance of their joy and their deep poverty abounded unto the riches of their liberality. For to their power, I bear record, yea, and beyond their power they were willing of themselves; Praying us with much intreaty that we would receive the gift, and take upon us the fellowship of the ministering to the saints. And this they did, not as we hoped, but first gave their own selves to the Lord, and unto us by the will of God."
(2 Corinthians 8:1-5)

"Being enriched in every thing to all bountifulness, which causeth through us thanksgiving to God. For the administration of this service not only supplieth the want of the saints, but is abundant also by many thanksgivings unto God; Whiles by the experiment of this ministration they glorify God for your professed subjection into the gospel of Christ, and for your liberal distribution unto them, and unto all men." *(2 Corinthians 9:11-13)*

As the Apostle Paul indicates in the above reference, the administration of the gift of giving not only meets the needs of others, it also honors and glorifies God as well.

Therefore

"As every man hath received the gift, even so minister the same one to another, as good stewards of the manifold grace of God." *(1 Peter 4:10)*

See additional reference. 1 Corinthians 12:4-11

The attitude of persons with this gift should be

- I am responsible for helping to support the work of the ministry. Romans 12:13
- I must be a free giver. Matthew 10:8
- I must be a generous giver. Luke 6:38

EXERCISE OBEDIENCE TO YOUR SPIRITUAL GIFT

Many have this gift but are not exercising it because of reasons such as fear (2 Timothy 1:7; Psalms 34:4), unforgivingness (past hurts - Matthew 6:14), anger (Ephesians 4:26) and many others. In Proverbs 28:13, God says - He will not prosper you, if you cover your sins.

A few great financial givers of the Bible

- Children of Israel. Exodus 35:4-5, 36:5-7
- David. 1 Chronicles 29:1-20
- Solomon. 1 Kings 8:5,63; 2 Chronicles 1:6-12
- Widow woman. 1 Kings 17:8-16
- Shunammite woman. 2 Kings 4:8-17
- Widow woman. Mark 12:41-44
- Woman with alabaster box. Luke 7:36-47
- Zacchaeus. Luke 19:1-10
- Little boy. John 6:5-13
- Early church. Acts 2:44-46
- Dorcas. Acts 9:36-42
- Cornelius. Acts 10:1-31
- Lydia. Acts 16:14
- Paul. Acts 24:17
- Churches of Macedonia. 2 Corinthians 8:1-7
- Philippian church. Philippians 4:18

CHAPTER 12

Principle #12

DON'T HOARD IT

This is a sign of loving it - storing it up secretly. Remember, you can't hide anything from God. He is all knowing (Psalms 139; Proverbs 15:3; Hebrews 4:13; 1 John 3:20; Joshua 7:10,11,15,19-21,25,26; Acts 5:1-11).

"For the love of money is the root of all evil: which while some coveted after, they have erred from the faith, and pierced themselves through with many sorrows." *(1 Timothy 6:10)*

If you keep more than what's right, you lose

"For riches are not for ever: and doth the crown endure to every generation?" *(Proverbs 27:24)*

"Remove far from me vanity and lies: give me neither poverty nor riches; feed me with food convenient for me: Lest I be full, and deny thee, and say, Who is the Lord? or lest I be poor, and steal, and take the name of my God in vain." *(Proverbs 30:8-9)*

"There is that maketh himself rich, yet hath nothing: there is that maketh himself poor, yet hath great riches." *(Proverbs 13:7)*

Read the parable of the rich fool. Luke 12:13-21,31,34

"Will a man rob God? Yet ye have robbed me. But ye say, Wherein have we robbed thee? In tithes and offerings." *(Malachi 3:8)*

"There is a sore evil which I have seen under the sun, namely, riches kept for the owners thereof to their hurt. But those riches perish by evil travail: and he begetteth a son, and there is nothing in his hand. As he came forth of his mother's womb, naked shall he return to go as he came, and shall take nothing of his labour, which he may carry away in his hand." *(Ecclesiastes 5:13-15)*

See additional references.
James 5:3; Matthew 6:19-20; 2 Corinthians 8:15, 9:6; Galatians 6:7-8; 1 Timothy 6:17-18

God does not esteem (highly regard) riches

"Will he esteem thy riches? no, not gold, nor all the forces of strength." *(Job 36:19)*

See additional references. Job 34:19; Proverbs 22:2;Ecclesiastes 10:6; Luke 1:53

If you give, you gain

"There is that scattereth, and yet increaseth; and there is that withholdeth more than is meet, but it tendeth to poverty. He that withholdeth corn, the people shall curse him: but blessing shall be upon the head of him that selleth it."
(Proverbs 11:24,26)

"There is that maketh himself rich, yet hath nothing: there is that maketh himself poor, yet hath great riches." *(Proverbs 13:7)*

"Better is an handful with quietness, than both the hands full with travail and vexation of spirit."
(Ecclesiastes 4:6)

"Give, and it shall be given unto you; good measure, pressed down, and shaken together, and running over, shall men give into your bosom. For with the same measure that ye mete withal it shall be measured to you again." *(Luke 6:38)*

A righteous person must be content with what they have, until God gives the increase.

"But godliness with contentment is great gain."
(1 Timothy 6:6)

"Better is little with the fear of the Lord than great treasure and trouble therewith." *(Proverbs 15:16)*

"Better is a little with righteousness than great revenues without right." *(Proverbs 16:8)*

See also. Psalms 37:16, 41:1-3

Paul said in the following reference, the spirit of contentment builds character.

"But I rejoiced in the Lord greatly, that now at the last your care of me hath flourished again; wherein ye were also careful, but ye lacked opportunity. Not that I speak in respect of want: for I have learned, in whatsoever state I am, therewith to be content. I know both how to be abased, and I know how to abound: every where and in all things I am instructed both to be full and to be hungry, both to abound and to suffer need. I can do all things through Christ which strengtheneth me." *(Philippians 4:10-13)*

You should do all things in view of the salvation and the transformation of souls. See 1 Corinthians 10:33 and 1 Corinthians 9:19-23. When you do, you are glorifying God (1 Corinthians 10:31). If not, you are glorifying the devil. Read again the story of the rich fool in Luke 12:16-21.

CHAPTER 13

Principle #13

DON'T WASTE IT

To waste means to mis-manage

"When they were filled, he said unto his disciples, Gather up the fragments that remain, that nothing be lost." *(John 6:12)*

Don't take the work of your hands and waste it on works of the flesh. This is a sign of living after the flesh, not after the Spirit. When you do this, you are living a fleshly life, not a spiritual life. When you waste your blessings, you are being carnally minded, not spiritually minded (Isaiah 55:2).

"Therefore, brethren, we are debtors, not to the flesh, to live after the flesh. For if ye live after the flesh, ye shall die: but if ye through the Spirit do mortify the deeds of the body, ye shall live. For as many as are led by the Spirit of God, they are the sons of God. For ye have not received the spirit of bondage again to fear; but ye have received the Spirit of adoption, whereby we cry, Abba, Father."
(Romans 8:12-15)

"For he that soweth to his flesh shall of the flesh reap corruption; but he that soweth to the Spirit shall of the Spirit reap life everlasting." *(Galatians 6:8)*

The holy portion belongs to God. Leviticus 27:30,32

"It is a snare to the man who devoureth that which is holy, and after vows to make enquiry."
(Proverbs 20:25)

"There is treasure to be desired and oil in the dwelling of the wise; but a foolish man spendeth it up." *(Proverbs 21:20)*

See additional references. Proverbs 21:17; James 4:4; Galatians 5:9; Romans 6:19; 1 Timothy 5:6

Stay away from get-rich-quick schemes

"He that tilleth his land shall be satisfied with bread: but he that followeth vain persons is void of under-standing."*(Proverbs 12:11)* See also. Proverbs 13:11

"For before these days rose up Theudas, boasting himself to be somebody; to whom a number of men, about four hundred, joined themselves: who was slain; and all, as many as obeyed him, were scattered, and brought to nought. After this man rose up Judas of Galilee in the days of the taxing, and drew away much people after him: he also perished; and all, even as many as obeyed him, were dispersed."
(Acts 5:36-37)

"The simple believeth every word: but the prudent man looketh well to his going." *(Proverbs 14:15)*

"Also, that the soul be without knowledge, it is not good; and he that hasteth with his feet sinneth." *(Proverbs 19:2)*   Beware of thieves. Proverbs 29:24

"He that answereth a matter before he heareth it, it is folly and shame unto him." *(Proverbs 21:5)*

"He that tilleth his land shall have plenty of bread: but he that followeth after vain persons shall have poverty enough. A faithful man shall abound with blessings: but he that maketh haste to be rich shall not be innocent." *(Proverbs 28:19-20)*

"As he came forth of his mother's womb, naked shall he return to go as he came, and shall take nothing of his labour, which he may carry away in his hand. And this also is a sore evil, that in all points as he came, so shall he go: and what profit hath he that hath laboured for the wind? All his days also he eateth in darkness, and he hath much sorrow and wrath with his sickness." *(Ecclesiastes 5:15-17)*

Gambling. This is a spirit of unrighteous covetousness – a strong desire to satisfy a deep hunger of wanting more. This sin is also known as a spirit of avarice (greed). Even winning will not satisfy you.

"He that loveth silver shall not be satisfied with silver; nor he that loveth abundance with increase: this is also vanity." *(Ecclesiastes 5:10)* **Answer. Ps. 107:9**

Therefore, put off the old man

"Mortify therefore your members which are upon the earth; fornication, uncleanness, inordinate affection, evil concupiscence, and covetousness, which is idolatry." *(Colossians 3:5)*

If not - the result

"For this ye know, that no whoremonger, nor unclean person, nor covetous man, who is an idolater, hath any inheritance in the kingdom of Christ and of God." *(Ephesians 5:5)* God's final wrath. Revelation 21:8

"Thou shalt have no other gods before me." *(Exodus 20:3)*

Don't fall for this temptation

"But they that will be rich fall into temptation and a snare, and into many foolish and hurtful lusts, which drown men in destruction and perdition." *(1 Timothy 6:9)* Remember Solomon. Prov. 30:8-9

"Wealth gotten by vanity shall be diminished: but he that gathereth by labour shall increase."
(Proverbs 13:11)

"Let your conversation be without covetousness; and be content with such things as ye have: for he hath said, I will never leave thee, nor forsake thee."
(Hebrews 13:5)

Gambling should be hated and rejected by all of God's children, as Paul indicated. See Psalms 10:3.

"I have coveted no man's silver, or gold, or apparel."
(Acts 20:33)   Dishonest gain. Jeremiah 22:17 AMP

"But ye are they that forsake the Lord, that forget my holy mountain, that prepare a table for that troop, and that furnish the drink offering unto that number."
(Isaiah 65:11)

Other references. Exodus 20:17; Proverbs 8:36, 10:2, 12:3,11,15:27,22:16; Ecclesiastes 2:3,8,10,11,8:17;Luke 15:11-30; John 6:12; 1 Corinthians 6:12,8:9,13; Galatians 5:23;   Ephesians 3:20, 4:28, 5:3; 2 Thessalonians 3:12; Philippians 4:19; 1 Timothy 5:22; 1 Corinthians 6:9-10; Jeremiah 17:11; James 4:4; 1 John 2:15-16; Galatians 5:16; Psalms 119:36; Ezekiel 33:31; Isaiah 33:15; 1 Tim. 6:10; Heb. 13:5-6; Habakkuk 2:9-11

Unbelievers support sin, believers support right-eousness (Amos 5:25-27).   You must stop giving

DON'T WASTE IT

God's money to the world (Hosea 2:8-10).

Warning for church leaders (Titus 1:7;1 Timothy 3:8).

Read chapter 1 again on acquiring money honestly.

God does not want you to waste financial resources on anything like drugs, cigarettes and alcohol.

"Know ye not that ye are the temple of God, and that the Spirit of God dwelleth in you? If any man defile the temple of God, him shall God destroy; for the temple of God is holy, which temple ye are."
(1 Corinthians 3:16-17)

"What? know ye not that your body is the temple of the Holy Ghost which is in you, which ye have of God, and ye are not your own? For ye are bought with a price: therefore glorify God in your body, and in your spirit, which are God's."
(1 Corinthians 6:19-20)

"But take heed lest by any means this liberty of yours become a stumblingblock to them that are weak." *(1 Corinthians 8:9)*

See references. Romans 2:14,14:13,16; Hebrews 12:1; 1 Corinthians 6:12-13; Ephesians 5:7,17;   1 Peter 5:8

If you are not placing God's house first with your finances, you are simply wasting them. Read chapters 1 & 2 of Haggai for the right priority with money.

CHAPTER 14

Principle #14

DON'T WORSHIP IT

Worshipping anyone or anything other than God
makes you an idolater

God's warning of worshipping the idol god of silver and gold

"Thou shalt have no other gods before me.
Thou shalt not make unto thee any graven image,
or any likeness of any thing that is in heaven
above, or that is in the earth beneath, or that is in
the water under the earth."
(Exodus 20:3-4)

"Thou shalt make thee no molten gods."
(Exodus 34:17)

This leads to death

"Their idols are silver and gold, the work of men's
hands. They have mouths, but they speak not: eyes
have they, but they see not: They have ears, but

they hear not: noses have they,   but they smell not: They have hands, but they handle not: feet have they, but they walk not: neither speak they through their throat." *(Psalms 115:4-7)*

The future end to worshiping money

"In that day a man shall cast his idols of silver, and his idols of gold, which they made each one for him-self to worship, to the moles and to the bats." *(Isaiah 2:20)*

"Ye shall defile also the covering of thy graven images of silver, and the ornament of thy molten images of gold: thou shalt cast them away as a men-struous cloth; thou shalt say unto it, Get thee hence." *(Isaiah 30:22)*

"For in that day every man shall cast away his idols of silver, and his idols of gold, which your own hands have made unto you for a sin." *(Isaiah 31:7)*

"They have set up kings, but not by me: they have made princes, and I knew it not: of their silver and their gold have they made them idols, that they may be cut off." *(Hosea 8:4)*

The god of gold (apis - sacred bull) was one of the Egyptians chief gods.

In the world (Egypt), you worshiped such idol gods, but not anymore.

"Now therefore fear the Lord, and serve him in sincerity and in truth: and put away the gods which your fathers served on the other side of the flood, and in Egypt; and serve ye the Lord." *(Joshua 24:14)*

"But they rebelled against me, and would not hearken unto me: they did not every man cast away the abominations of their eyes, neither did they forsake the idols of Egypt: then I said, I will pour out my fury upon them to accomplish my anger against them in the midst of the land of Egypt." *(Ezekiel 20:8)*

Israel's breaking of God's covenant

"And when the people saw that Moses delayed to come down out of the mount, the people gathered themselves together unto Aaron, and said unto him, Up, make us gods, which shall go before us; for as for this Moses, the man that brought us up out of the land of Egypt, we wot not what is become of him. And Aaron said unto them, Break off the golden earrings, which are in the ears of your wives, of your sons, and of your daughters, and bring them unto me. And all the people brake off the golden earrings which were in their ears, and brought them unto Aaron. And he received them at their hand, and fashioned it with a graving tool, after he had made it a molten calf: and they said, These be thy gods, O Israel, which brought thee up out of the land of Egypt.   And when Aaron saw it, he built an altar before it; and Aaron made proclamation, and said, To morrow is a feast to the Lord.   And they rose up early on the morrow, and offered burnt offerings, and brought peace offerings; and the people sat down to eat and to drink, and rose up to play.

And the Lord said unto Moses, Go, get thee down; for thy people, which thou broughtest out of the land of Egypt, have corrupted themselves: They have turned aside quickly out of the way which I commanded them: they have made them a molten calf, and have worshipped it, and have sacrificed thereunto, and said, These be thy gods, O Israel, which have brought thee up out of the land of Egypt." *(Exodus 32:1-8)*

Remember God's warning in Exodus 20:23,22:20.

They died instantly @ the moment of judgment

"And Moses turned, and went down from the mount, and the two tables of the testimony were in his hand: the tables were written on both their sides; on the one side and on the other were they written. And it came to pass, as soon as he came nigh unto the camp, that he saw the calf, and the dancing: and

Moses' anger waxed hot, and he cast the tables out of his hands, and brake them beneath the mount. And when Moses saw that the people were naked; (for Aaron had made them naked unto their shame among their enemies:) Then Moses stood in the gate of the camp, and said, Who is on the Lord's side? let him come unto me. And all the sons of Levi gathered themselves together unto him. And he said unto them, Thus saith the Lord God of Israel, Put every man his sword by his side, and go in and out from gate to gate throughout the camp, and slay every man his brother, and every man his companion, and every man his neighbour. And the children of Levi did according to the word of Moses: and there fell of the people that day about three thousand men." *(Exodus 32:15,19,25-28)*

See additional references. Exodus 31:1-8; Deuteronomy 9:16-21; Nehemiah 9:18

This worshipping took place in the city of Memphis near Goshen.

You must remain steadfast in your faith and never worship the golden image - even upon death. See the story of the Hebrew boys (Daniel 3:1-30).

See the following New Testament example of God's immediate judgement of worshipping money.

Death of Sapphira & Ananias

"But a certain man named Ananias, with Sapphira his wife, sold a possession, And kept back part of the price, his wife also being privy to it, and brought a certain part, and laid it at the apostles' feet. But Peter said, Ananias, why hath Satan filled thine heart to lie to the Holy Ghost, and to keep back part of the price of the land? Whiles it remained, was it not thine own? and after it was sold, was it not in thine own power? why hast thou conceived this thing in thine heart? thou hast not lied unto men, but unto God. And Ananias hearing these words fell down, and gave up the ghost: and great fear came on all them that heard these things. And the young men arose, wound him up, and carried him out, and buried him. And it was about the space of three hours after, when his wife, not knowing what was done, came in. And Peter answered unto her, Tell me whether ye sold the land for so much? And she said, Yea, for so much. Then Peter said unto her, How is it that ye have agreed together to tempt the Spirit of the Lord? behold, the feet of them which have buried thy husband are at the door, and shall carry thee out. Then fell she down straightway at his feet, and yielded up the ghost: and the young men came in, and found her dead, and, carrying her forth, buried her by her husband. And great fear came upon all the church, and upon as many as heard these things." *(Acts 5:1-11)*

Future judgement of all concealed things. Romans 2:16; 1 Corinthians 4:5; Ecclesiastes 12:14

Why not come clean with God now (Proverbs 28:13).

Signs of worshipping money

- *Serving it*. 1 Timothy 6:9; Matthew 6:24

- *Boastful spirit*. Deuteronomy 8:17-18; Jeremiah 9:23-24; 1 Timothy 6:4-19; James 4:16

- *Selfish spirit*. Mark 10:17-27; 1 Timothy 6:17-19; 1 John 3:17; Luke 12:16-21

- *Trusting it*. This is false hope. Deuteronomy 8:17-18; Proverbs 3:5-6. Money will fail you by itself. Proverbs 11:4,28; Ecclesiastes 7:12; Luke 16:9;Zephaniah 1:18;1 Peter 1:7;2 Peter 3:10-13; Job 31:24,25,28; Habakkuk 2:18-20 (no profit)

- *Bad attitude*. Deuteronomy 8:17; 1 Timothy 6:17-18; James 1:10

- *Hoarding it*. Setting aside for selfish reasons. See chapter on don't hoard it.

- *Coveting it*.This is a lusting spirit. An unrighteous desire for something. Romans 13:13-14; Exodus 20:4; Deuteronomy 4:15-16; Luke 12:15; Colossians 3:5; 1 Corinthians 6:9-10

DON'T WORSHIP IT

- *Love it*. Deuteronomy 8:18-19; 1 Timothy 6:9-10, 17; Ecclesiastes 5:10-12; Luke 12:16-21,18:18-24

- *Can't acquire enough*. Ecclesiastes 5:10-12; Luke12:15-21, 16:13; 1 Timothy 6:6,9

- *Do anything for it*. Lying (2 Kings 5:20-27); Robbing God (Malachi 3:7-8; Joshua 7:20,21); Labouring to be rich (Proverbs 23:4, 1 Timothy 6:9); Oppressing the less fortunate (James 2:6); Making merchandise of people (2 Peter 2:3)

- *Forgetting God*. Deuteronomy 8:12-14, 31:20, 32:15; Hosea 13:6;Prov. 30:8-9;Matthew 19:21-22

- *Esteem it more than God*. You have to be delivered from this spirit. Job 20:15; Jeremiah 44:28; Colossians 3:2-6; 1 Peter 1:7; Luke 18:18-24

Worshipping the golden image of money will destroy you, if you are not delivered from it (Amos 8:14; 1 Kings 12:25-30; Hosea 8:4; Revelation 20:4,21:8).

This sin causes you to miss the kingdom of God (1 Cor. 6:9-10; Gal. 5:19-21). You must remain faithful like Abraham did. He never allowed his material possessions to become idolatrous. Jesus did not worship the kingdom of riches, neither should you (Matthew 4:8-10). The final judgement for idols and those who worship them (Isaiah 31:7,44:9,11; Jeremiah 51:18). Other references. Isaiah 2:20,30:22 AMP; Hosea 14:3

CHAPTER 15
Principle #15
DON'T TRUST IT

The only gold you should place your trust in - is that which has been tried by fire - God's word (Psalms 12:6-7, 19:7-10; Revelation 3:18).

Trusting in money is a fool's confidence

"If I have made gold my hope, or have said to the fine gold, Thou art my confidence; If I rejoiced because my wealth was great, and because mine hand had gotten much; This also were an iniquity to be punished by the judge: for I should have denied the God that is above." *(Job 31:24,25,28)*

Trusting in God is a wise person's confidence

"By terrible things in righteousness wilt thou answer us, O God of our salvation; who art the confidence of all the ends of the earth, and of them that are afar off upon the sea." *(Psalms 65:5)*

"In the fear of the Lord is strong confidence: and his children shall have a place of refuge."
(Proverbs 14:26)

DON'T TRUST IT

Who to put your trust in

The true and living God

"Every word of God is pure: he is a shield unto them that put their trust in him." *(Proverbs 30:5)*

Always remember, God is your source - everything else is a resource (2 Corinthians 3:5).

"Who being the brightness of his glory, and the express image of his person, and upholding all things by the word of his power, when he had by himself purged our sins, sat down on the right hand of the Majesty on high." *(Hebrews 1:3)*

"For in him we live, and move, and have our being; as certain also of your own poets have said, For we are also his offspring." *(Acts 17:28)*

God's way is perfect (2 Samuel 22:31).

Especially the rich

"Charge them that are rich in this world, that they be not highminded, nor trust in uncertain riches, but in the living God, who giveth us richly all things to enjoy." *(1 Timothy 6:17)*

Esteem the wisdom of God above money

"For wisdom is a defence, and money is a defence: but the excellency of knowledge is, that wisdom giveth life to them that have it." *(Ecclesiastes 7:11-12)*

"Man that is in honour, and understandeth not, is like the beasts that perish." *(Psalms 49:20)*

"Happy is the man that findeth wisdom, and the man that getteth understanding. For the merchandise of it is better than the merchandise of silver, and the gain thereof than fine gold. She is more precious than rubies: and all the things thou canst desire are not to be compared unto her. Length of days is in her right hand; and in her left hand riches and honour. Her ways are ways of pleasantness, and all her paths are peace. She is a tree of life to them that lay hold upon her: and happy is every one that retaineth her." *(Proverbs 3:13-18)*   See also. Proverbs 2:7

Money is temporary

"From men which are thy hand, O Lord, from men of the world, which have their portion in this life, and whose belly thou fillest with thy hid treasure: they are full of children, and leave the rest of their substance to their babes." *(Psalms 17:14)*

DON'T TRUST IT

Other references. Proverbs 10:8,12:15, 14:16,15:5

"For riches are not for ever: and doth the crown endure to every generation?" *(Proverbs 27:24)*

  Your money is limited to this life. You must realize that money has wings. It will soon fly away.

Which type of wings do you put your trust in ?

Wrong wings (Wings of money)!

"Wilt thou set thine eyes upon that which is not? for riches certainly make themselves wings; they fly away as an eagle toward heaven." *(Proverbs 23:5)*

Right wings (Wings of God)!

"How excellent is thy lovingkindness, O God! therefore the children of men put their trust under the shadow of thy wings." *(Psalms 36:7)*

"To the chief Musician, Altaschith, Michtam of David, when he fled from Saul in the cave. Be merciful unto me, O God, be merciful unto me: for my soul trusteth in thee: yea, in the shadow of thy wings will I make my refuge, until these calamities be overpast." *(Psalms 57:1)*

"I will abide in thy tabernacle for ever: I will trust in the covert of thy wings. Selah." *(Psalms 61:4)*

"He shall cover thee with his feathers, and under his wings shalt thou trust: his truth shall be thy shield and buckler." *(Psalms 91:4)*

"The Lord recompense thy work, and a full reward be given thee of the Lord God of Israel, under whose wings thou art come to trust." *(Ruth 2:12)*

Can't fully protect you

The mind set of many who have money - they think that it is their wall of protection. Read Romans 12:3

"The rich man's wealth is his strong city, and as an high wall in his own conceit." *(Proverbs 18:11)*
See Isaiah 26:1, Zechariah 2:5, Psalms 18:2-3 and Isaiah 60:18 (spiritual wall) for true protection.

"The fear of man bringeth a snare: but whoso putteth his trust in the Lord shall be safe." *(Proverbs 29:25)*

"When thou criest, let thy companies deliver thee; but the wind shall carry them all away; vanity shall take them: but he that putteth his trust in me shall possess the land, and shall inherit my holy mountain." *(Isaiah 57:13)*

DON'T TRUST IT

Can't save you

"The Lord redeemeth the soul of his servants: and none of them that trust in him shall be desolate." *(Psalms 34:22)*

"And the Lord shall help them and deliver them: he shall deliver them from the wicked, and save them, because they trust in him." *(Psalms 37:40)*

"They that trust in their wealth, and boast themselves in the multitude of their riches; None of them can by any means redeem his brother, nor give to God a ransom for him." *(Psalms 49:6-7)*

Read the story of the parable of the rich young man in Luke 12:13-21.

Can't keep you

"Who are kept by the power of God through faith unto salvation ready to be revealed in the last time." *(1 Peter 1:5)*

See additional references. 2 Timothy 3:15; 1 John 1:7

"But the Lord is faithful, who shall stablish you, and keep you from evil."   *(2 Thessalonians 3:3)*

"Now unto him that is able to keep you from falling, and to present you faultless before the presence of his glory with exceeding joy, To the only wise God our Saviour, be glory and majesty, dominion and power, both now and ever. Amen." *(Jude 1:24-25)*

Trusting in money is usually a stumbling block to unbelievers and baby Christians

"Labour not to be rich: cease from thine own wisdom. Wilt thou set thine eyes upon that which is not? for riches certainly make themselves wings; they fly away as an eagle toward heaven."
(Proverbs 23:4-5)

"When the wicked are multiplied, transgression increaseth: but the righteous shall see their fall."
(Proverbs 29:6)

   The knowledge of God's wisdom will guide your footsteps (Psalms 127:1, 119:105, 119:42,72,127, 160; Proverbs 24:3-4, 8:10,11,18,19,20,21).

You must learn how to put your trust in God's word.

Will not deliver you in time of God's wrath

"The integrity of the upright shall guide them: but the perverseness of transgressors shall destroy them. Riches profit not in the day of wrath: but righteousness delivereth from death. The righteousness of the perfect shall direct his way: but the wicked shall fall by his own wickedness. The righteousness of the upright shall deliver them: but transgressors shall be taken in their own naughtiness. When a wicked man dieth, his expectation shall perish: and the hope of unjust men perisheth. The righteous is delivered out of trouble, and the wicked cometh in his stead." *(Proverbs 11:3-8)*

"Neither their silver nor their gold shall be able to deliver them in the day of the Lord's wrath; but the whole land shall be devoured by the fire of his jealousy: for he shall make even a speedy riddance of all them that dwell in the land." *(Zephaniah 1:18)*

See additional references. Revelation 3:5, 6:15-17, 20:12,15

Only true faith will deliver you at the appearing of Jesus (1 Peter 1:7).

Remember, money can and will fail you (Genesis 47:15; Revelation 13:17, 14:8, 18:2).

WHAT TO-DO WITH MONEY

Trusting in money (silver & gold) is a practice of heathens (non-believers) Psalms 135:15-18.

Can't take it with you @ death

"Then Job arose, and rent his mantle, and shaved his head, and fell down upon the ground, and worshipped, And said, Naked came I out of my mother's womb, and naked shall I return thither: the Lord gave, and the Lord hath taken away; blessed be the name of the Lord." *(Job 1:20-21)*

"They take the timbrel and harp, and rejoice at the sound of the organ. They spend their days in wealth, and in a moment go down to the grave." *(Job 21:12-13)*

"For he seeth that wise men die, likewise the fool and the brutish person perish, and leave their wealth to others. Be not thou afraid when one is made rich, when the glory of his house is increased; For when he dieth he shall carry nothing away: his glory shall not descend after him." *(Psalms 49:10,16,17)*

"A good man leaveth an inheritance to his children's children: and the wealth of the sinner is laid up for the just." *(Proverbs 13:22)*

DON'T TRUST IT

The story of a rich man

"And he said unto them, Take heed, and beware of covetousness: for a man's life consisteth not in the abundance of the things which he possesseth. And he spake a parable unto them, saying, The ground of a certain rich man brought forth plentifully: And he thought within himself, saying, What shall I do, because I have no room where to bestow my fruits? And he said, This will I do: I will pull down my barns, and build greater; and there will I bestow all my fruits and my goods. And I will say to my soul, Soul, thou hast much goods laid up for many years; take thine ease, eat, drink, and be merry. But God said unto him, Thou fool, this night thy soul shall be required of thee: then whose shall those things be, which thou hast provided? So is he that layeth up treasure for himself, and is not rich toward God."
(Luke 12:15-21)

Remember to put your trust - only in the Lord

"The Lord is good, a strong hold in the day of trouble; and he knoweth them that trust in him."
(Nahum 1:7)

Do not put your trust in the world's way (Isaiah 30:1-3), if you do, it will surely bring you to shame.

"Some trust in chariots, and some in horses: but we will remember the name of the Lord our God." *(Psalms 20:7)* The results. Psalms 20:8

"Trust in him at all times; ye people, pour out your heart before him: God is a refuge for us. Selah." *(Psalms 62:8)*

"They that trust in the Lord shall be as mount Zion, which cannot be removed, but abideth for ever." *(Psalms 125:1)* See also. Psalms 84:12

"He that trusteth in his riches shall fall: but the righteous shall flourish as a branch." *(Proverbs 11:28)*

"Thou wilt keep him in perfect peace, whose mind is stayed on thee: because he trusteth in thee." *(Isaiah 26:3)*

"The Lord is my rock, and my fortress, and my deliverer; my God, my strength, in whom I will trust; my buckler, and the horn of my salvation, and my high tower." *(Psalms 18:2)*

Read Jeremiah 48:4-8, for God's judgement on Moab.

See other references. 2 Samuel 22:3,31; Job 35:14; Psalms 19:14,18:30,57:2; Isaiah 26:4; Genesis 15:1; Revelation 18:2; 1 Chronicles 28:20; Matthew 28:20; Deuteronomy 32:36-39; Psalms 22:4-5

DON'T TRUST IT

Trusting your old unregenerated heart is false trust

"The heart is deceitful above all things, and desperately wicked: who can know it?" *(Jeremiah 17:9)*

"For this people's heart is waxed gross, and their ears are dull of hearing, and their eyes they have closed; lest at any time they should see with their eyes, and hear with their ears, and should understand with their heart, and should be converted, and I should heal them." *(Matthew 13:15)*

"But ye have not so learned Christ; If so be that ye have heard him, and have been taught by him, as the truth is in Jesus: That ye put off concerning the former conversation the old man, which is corrupt according to the deceitful lusts; And be renewed in the spirit of your mind; And that ye put on the new man, which after God is created in righteousness and true holiness." *(Ephesians 4:20-24)*

Trusting in the true and living God is true trust

"Blessed is the man that trusteth in the Lord, and whose hope the Lord is." *(Jeremiah 17:7)*

"And ye are complete in him, which is the head of all principality and power." *(Colossians 2:10)*

CHAPTER 16
Principle #16

ENJOY IT

"Thou art worthy, O Lord, to receive glory and honour and power: for thou hast created all things, and for thy pleasure they are and were created." *(Revelation 4:11)* To His glory. 1 Corinthians 10:31

"If they obey and serve him, they shall spend their days in prosperity, and their years in pleasures." *(Job 36:11)* See also. Psalms 84:11; Proverbs 15:6

"Be not thou afraid when one is made rich, when the glory of his house is increased." *(Psalms 49:16)*

Make friends

"Wealth maketh many friends; but the poor is separated from his neighbour." *(Proverbs 19:4)*

Solomon said

"There is nothing better for a man, than that he should eat and drink, and that he should make his soul enjoy good in his labour. This also I saw, that it was from the hand of God." *(Ecclesiastes 2:24)*

ENJOY IT

"And also that every man should eat and drink, and enjoy the good of all his labour, it is the gift of God." *(Ecclesiastes 3:13)*

"Behold that which I have seen: it is good and comely for one to eat and to drink, and to enjoy the good of all his labour that he taketh under the sun all the days of his life, which God giveth him: for it is his portion. Every man also to whom God hath given riches and wealth, and hath given him power to eat thereof, and to take his portion, and to rejoice in his labour; this is the gift of God. For he shall not much remember the days of his life; because God answereth him in the joy of his heart."
(Ecclesiastes 5:18-20) But cherish God more!

"Consider the work of God: for who can make that straight, which he hath made crooked? In the day of prosperity be joyful, but in the day of adversity consider: God also hath set the one over against the other, to the end that man should find nothing after him." *(Ecclesiastes 7:13-14)* Read. Ecclesiastes 9:7

Remember to exercise self control.

"And God is able to make all grace abound toward you; that ye, always having all sufficiency in all things, may abound to every good work: Being enriched in every thing to all bountifulness, which

causeth through us thanksgiving to God."
(2 Corinthians 9:8,11)

"Charge them that are rich in this world, that they be not highminded, nor trust in uncertain riches, but in the living God, who giveth us richly all things to enjoy; That they do good, that they be rich in good works, ready to distribute, willing to communicate." *(1 Timothy 6:17-18)*

Never enjoy money to the point of sinning

"And take heed to yourselves, lest at any time your hearts be overcharged with surfeiting, and drunkenness, and cares of this life, and so that day come upon you unawares. For as a snare shall it come on all them that dwell on the face of the whole earth." *(Luke 21:34-35)*

Surfeiting - oppressing your system by intemperate or self indulgence in things such as eating, drinking and riotous type living.

Drunkenness. 1 Corinthians 6:9-10; Galatians 5:21; Proverbs 20:1; Romans 13:13; Isaiah 28:7

Riotous and lose living (sensual living - worldly activities, James 3:15) along with vanity (emptiness) and folly (foolishness, silliness) Ecclesiastes 2:1-3,10,11; 1 Kings 3:3, 11:1-11; Hebrews 11:24-26.

CONCLUSION

Don't forget God

Deuteronomy 8:10-20, 26:5-11

The conclusion of the matter

"So then every one of us shall give account of himself to God." *(Romans 14:12)*

"And the Lord said, Who then is that faithful and wise steward, whom his lord shall make ruler over his household, to give them their portion of meat in due season? Blessed is that servant, whom his lord when he cometh shall find so doing."
(Luke 12:42-43)

The parable of the pounds

"And it came to pass, that when he was returned, having received the kingdom, then he commanded these servants to be called unto him, to whom he had given the money, that he might know how much every man had gained by trading. Then came the first, saying, Lord, thy pound hath gained ten pounds. And he said unto him, Well, thou good servant: because thou hast been faithful in a very little,

have thou authority over ten cities. And the second came, saying, Lord, thy pound hath gained five pounds. And he said likewise to him, Be thou also over five cities. And another came, saying, Lord, behold, here is thy pound, which I have kept laid up in a napkin: For I feared thee, because thou art an austere man: thou takest up that thou layedst not down, and reapest that thou didst not sow. And he saith unto him, Out of thine own mouth will I judge thee, thou wicked servant. Thou knewest that I was an austere man, taking up that I laid not down, and reaping that I did not sow: Wherefore then gavest not thou my money into the bank, that at my coming I might have required mine own with usury? And he said unto them that stood by, Take from him the pound, and give it to him that hath ten pounds. (And they said unto him, Lord, he hath ten pounds.) For I say unto you, That unto every one which hath shall be given; and from him that hath not, even that he hath shall be taken away from him. But those mine enemies, which would not that I should reign over them, bring hither, and slay them before me."
(Luke 19:15-27)

"And Jesus answered and said unto him, Blessed art thou, Simon Barjona: for flesh and blood hath not revealed it unto thee, but my Father which is in heaven." *(Matthew 16:17)*

CONCLUSION

Words of Solomon

"Let us hear the conclusion of the whole matter: Fear God, and keep his commandments: for this is the whole duty of man. For God shall bring every work into judgment, with every secret thing, whether it be good, or whether it be evil."
(Ecclesiastes 12:13-14)

Words of Jesus

"And he said also unto his disciples, There was a certain rich man, which had a steward; and the same was accused unto him that he had wasted his goods. And he called him, and said unto him, How is it that I hear this of thee? give an account of thy steward-ship; for thou mayest be no longer steward."
(Luke 16:1-2)

Now that you have finished reading this book, you should have identified the various principles you have been omitting or not properly keeping. Therefore, you must confess and/or repent (Proverbs 28:13; 1 John 1:9; James 4:17) and use the principles in this book to help you walk in faith-fulness to God in financial stewardship - and begin to enjoy His liberty and many blessings (Psalms 119:44-45; Job 36:11).   **A-men´**

NOTES

Other Books by Robert Mukes

Things Money Can't Buy®

This book reveals 31 things that money can't buy. If you desire to learn the true riches of God, this is the book to read.   (218 Pages)

To order:
Send $19.95 + $6.00 Shipping & Handling
Robert Mukes Ministries
3125 S. Mendenhall #306 Memphis, TN 38115

The Need Meeter™

  This book teaches you that God is your provider. You will learn your covenant responsibilities and God's eight (8) ways of meeting your financial needs and how to receive the desires of your heart.
(74 Pages)

To order:
Send $9.95 + $4.00 Shipping & Handling
Robert Mukes Ministries
3125 S. Mendenhall #306 Memphis, TN 38115

NOTES

Made in the USA
Charleston, SC
08 January 2014